TEACHING FOR SURVIVAL

Mark Terry

Foreword by Garrett Hardin

A FRIENDS OF THE EARTH / BALLANTINE BOOK
An Intext Publisher
NEW YORK

Copyright © 1971 by Mark Terry

SBN 345-02120-7-125

All rights reserved.

First Printing: January, 1971

Printed in the United States of America

BALLANTINE BOOKS, Inc.
101 Fifth Avenue, New York, N.Y. 10003

ALL EDUCATION IS ENVIRONMENTAL EDUCATION.

The pleas for development of environmental education as a new subject have misrepresented the problem, which is to change the environmental education that is provided in the study of any subject and in any classroom according to our best understanding of environmental realities. We must realize that all educational situations contribute to environmental education. Environment is no single subject and is certainly not the property of a given teacher or classroom. Attempts to delegate responsibility for environmental education to such a teacher compound misunderstanding of the environment, which is dealt with in *every* teacher's classroom.

Mark Terry presents in TEACHING FOR SURVIVAL a way to change in the classroom the basic assumptions of our educational system—assumptions which ultimately lead to the destruction of our natural environment—and he clearly shows that the tools for change are, and always have been, at hand but we must learn to recognize and use them.

MORE BALLANTINE BOOKS
YOU WILL ENJOY

PLAY THERAPY, Virginia M. Axline $1.25
A landmark in its field, with specific illustrations of how therapy can be implemented in play contacts to aid the disturbed child. *400 pages with Index and 16 pages of illustrations.*

JORDI/LISA AND DAVID,
Dr. Theodore Isaac Rubin $.95
With insight and compassion a brilliant psychiatrist explores the secret world of the disturbed child.

THE POPULATION BOMB, Dr. Paul R. Ehrlich $.95
The national bestseller!
Overpopulation is now the dominant problem in all our personal, national, and international planning. Dr. Ehrlich clearly describes the dimensions of the crisis in all its aspects, and provides a realistic evaluation of the remaining options. *A Sierra Club/Ballantine Book*

MALABAR FARM, Louis Bromfield $1.25
The Pulitzer Prize author describes his success in the pioneering of organic farming methods on his famous farm in Ohio. Mr. Bromfield writes with a feeling for the countryside that is contagious.

THE ENVIRONMENTAL HANDBOOK: Prepared for the First National Environmental Teach-In—Edited by Garrett De Bell. *A Friends of the Earth/Ballantine Book* $.95
The 1970's is our last chance for a future that makes ecological sense. This handbook focuses on some of the major problems of our deteriorating environment, explains the nature of ecology and—most importantly—suggests action that can be taken right now in any community, by any individual.

To Order by mail, send price of book plus 5¢ for postage to Dept. CS, Ballantine Books, Inc., 36 West 20th Street, New York, New York 10003. Include your order with your address and zip code.

To the mountain lupine
after a light rain.

Contents

Foreword by Garrett Hardin		xi
Introduction:	The Need for Environmental Education	xv
Part One:	ENVIRONMENT AND EDUCATION	
Chapter One:	The Abundance of Environmental Educators	3
Chapter Two:	Overuse and Overgrowth	19
Part Two:	THE USES OF THE SCHOOL	
Chapter One:	The Classroom	49
Chapter Two:	The School	76
Chapter Three:	The District	107
Part Three:	THE SUBJECT MATTERS	
Chapter One:	The Observers	117
Chapter Two:	The Interpreters	142
Chapter Three:	The Users	163
Chapter Four:	Interdisciplinary Study	184
Conclusion:	Teaching for Survival	189
Bibliography		195

Acknowledgements

I would like to thank David Brower for being there and for listening in the spring of 1969 at the University of Washington. The continuing support and encouragement given me by Dave, Dr. Garrett Hardin, Perry Knowlton, and Ian Ballantine have made *Teaching for Survival* possible.

Teachers, teaching, and ecology have made a great deal more sense to me as a result of my contact with Walt Brautigan of Cornell University's Division of Science and Environmental Education. I would like to thank Walt, Dr. Anne LaBastille, also of Cornell, and Gray and Joyce Pedersen for reading parts of the manuscript.

Thanks also to my mother and father for many things, in particular for choosing to live on the Lake in sight of the Mountain; to my brother, for helping fill my environmental files; to Garth MacDonald for spending a day in Connecticut with the title; to Cynthia, Rick, Sinclair, Nick, Chris, Martha, Majors, and Nancy for sharing with me a year of biology while this book was brewing; and to Cathy, for staying with the book since before either of us knew there was to be a book.

Foreword

Garrett Hardin

A century after the word "ecology" was coined its subject matter became suddenly fashionable. Sudden popularity is always dangerous. Ecology now runs the risk of being suffocated by its friends—well-meaning friends it is true, but ones who are all too often ill-informed and generally poorly disciplined. The "Earth Day" of 22 April 1970 was in too many places paradoxically celebrated by an orgy of environmental littering, in the name of Environment. The ratio of emotion to analysis in the celebrations was perilously high.

Emotion is not wholly bad; in fact, we need a bit of it to get our engines of reform going. But it is doubtful if we should encourage the emotion of hatred of "the Establishment" or of anything else. We should always keep in mind the very real danger that we may become that which we hate. It is not hatred that we need now, but persistent determination, based on understanding.

Those who are in a position to teach, and to lead others to learn and act, can hardly find a better guide to environmental action than this richly detailed discussion by Mark Terry. This talented young teacher has modified the old saying "Charity begins at home," to read *Ecology begins at home*. Do not, he warns, set out to clean up the entire world at one fell swoop: you will certainly fail and be disillusioned. Instead, *look around you*. Open your ecological eyes, and you will see countless instances of environmental malfeasance taking place right in your own back yard. Some of the crimes will be delightfully easy to correct.

By tackling these first you will build up your political self-confidence—and thus ready yourself for tackling larger issues with an improved prospect of winning. It is not martyrdom but success that strengthens the will and quickens the reflexes.

To read *Teaching for Survival* word by word is to become irreversibly sensitized to one's immediate surroundings. The principal function of every artist is to make us see the world that was always there but which we were blindly unaware of until he opened our eyes. The artist creates that which has always existed. Mark Terry is such an artist, but one working in a new medium, environmental awareness. When an appreciable fraction of our population has had its eyes opened to this new vision the world will never be the same.

Let us hope this happens soon.

*TEACHING
FOR SURVIVAL*

Introduction:

The Need for Environmental Education

In 1893 the Committee of Ten report on secondary-school studies urged that botany teachers should take "an ecological approach" to their subject. Ten years later Liberty Hyde Bailey argued eloquently for general "nature study" throughout education. Environmental education, whether termed "ecology," "nature study," or some other name, was championed at nearly all the life science curriculum meetings held in this country since the turn of the century. Particularly the relationship of man to environment has been recognized as worthy of coverage in public-school curricula for generations.

The justifications given for this interest in environmental education have traditionally been two. In American public education, we educate to produce an enlightened electorate. For our representative democracy to function, our citizenry must be aware of and must understand their environment. The management of natural resources requires environmental understanding and participation on the part of the voting public. A certain amount of conservation education has long been recognized as necessary to meet this demand for an informed electorate.

The second major argument for environmental education has usually been the aesthetic. Appreciation of nature is somehow recognized as the rightful pursuit of the American citizen. Our mandate to secure the good life has included this enjoyment of the continent's natural wonders. The call for environmental education in the past has often been based on this need for the capacity to delight in nature.

With these main justifications, environmental education in one form or another has been subject to the same calls for development as the other subject areas. Education conferences have repeatedly suggested the need for environment textbooks, environment curriculum guides, and required environment units for teachers and students. Major developments following these suggestions have been slow in coming until recently.

The environmental revolution that has grown in the public mind through the final years of the sixties has ended the dormancy of efforts in environmental education. The pressures of population growth and environmental deterioration have grown fast enough to cause great concern for our present and future environmental health. The pressing of great amounts of environmental litigation has been accompanied by the entrance of environmental quality as a major political issue. Educators have renewed their calls for development of environmental education and have found an unusually attentive audience. Funds for environmental curricular development have begun flowing from federal, state, and private sources. Initial texts produced in the heat of this concern are already on the market and many more are in developmental stages. Special committees of state legislatures are seriously considering requirements of specified units of environmental study for students and for beginning teachers. A statement by the American Association of School Administrators, from their 1966 volume *Imperatives in Education*, typifies the concern with which the sudden upsurge in environmental education efforts is growing:

> As the prince in the ancient legend took the broken sword that the cringing knight had jealously broken in two and discarded and turned the tide of the battle, so must administrators and teachers—even when the circumstances are difficult—meet the challenge of instilling in the minds and hearts of a generation of

young people the understanding and commitment necessary to use the natural resources of this country successfully.

The Association's statement also typifies the problems that the environmental education movement is creating for itself. New curriculum development, student and teacher course requirements, assigning someone responsibility for environmental education, these are the actions most often and most eagerly proposed. The implication of such actions, proposals, and statements is that environmental education is a new and long-awaited development that must take its place in the traditional order of subject "coverage"; that someone can teach it as a subject; and that such education can cure our environmental ills. These implications indicate a misunderstanding of the nature of environmental education. This book is written with the hope of making clear this misunderstanding and of suggesting a different approach to environmental education.

In brief, my thesis is that all education is environmental education. The pleas for development of environmental education as a new subject have misrepresented the problem, which is to change the environmental education that is provided in the study of any subject and in any classroom according to our best understanding of environmental realities. We must realize that all educational situations contribute to environmental education. Environment is no single subject and is certainly not the property of a given teacher or classroom. Attempts to delegate responsibility for environmental education to such a teacher compound misunderstanding of the environment, which is dealt with in *every* teacher's classroom.

Though environmental education in schools can reasonably be expected to help our efforts to improve our environmental relationships, it should not be burdened with the unrealistic responsibility of stopping pollution or solving the deterioration of the environment. Aiming toward such goals tends to breed insensitivity to practical issues and to foster the growth of an already overwhelming rhetoric. A goal far more practical for schools and far more conducive to environmental education is to do all that is possible to improve the school's environmental relationships.

Suggestions are presented in the sections "The Uses of the School" and "The Subject Matters" for developing the potential of the school environment. The suggestions are not prescriptions. They are written to stimulate the thinking of teachers, administrators, and anyone interested along practical environmental lines. We must remember that we are not helpless in the face of environmental conditions; far from it. We are often the most dominant factor in creating the very conditions to which we object. It is particularly important for teachers to be sensitive to the degree to which they affect the environment of their classroom. We are perhaps the most adaptable of all "higher" animals; the range of actions available to each of us to improve our environmental relationships is limited only by our imaginations.

To suggest that this book is complete or definitive would be to perpetuate another environmental misunderstanding. In the Bibliography I have tried to spread the word about those projects and thinkers in environmental education, whether they employ that title or not, that have come to my attention. It is my hope that your use of this book and of others can be as much tempered by environmental sense as any other activity. The most important ideas for your classes will ultimately come from you. The environmental costs associated with the use of your own imagination are far less than those attached to the publication of this or any other book. If you find books useful, it is my sincere hope that you will open communication with your fellow educators and students and pass both the word and the books along.

Earlier I mentioned the two traditional justifications for environmental education: the need for an educated electorate and the need for appreciation of nature. A measure of the coming of age of environmental understanding will be the extent to which a new need for environmental education is recognized. This need incorporates the previous two but is at once more general and more realistic. Before we are citizens in a representative democracy and before we are beings capable of appreciating nature, we are nature ourselves and are participants in the natural world. The need for environmental education, education concerning environmental principles and their applications, emanates from our extraordinary power to affect the natural environment. Animals and plants less capable of forcing environmental alterations are generally less conscious of environmental problems. Instincts take care of population problems for some species; catastrophes unlamented take care of similar problems for others. Our capacity for altering environmental conditions is accompanied by a capacity for sensing values. Less controlled by instincts, we do not settle for catastrophe if we can help it. Values once oriented toward unlimited growth must now be tempered by our growing environmental understanding. The need for this reorientation of values *is* the need for environmental re-education. Freedom, in this case freedom from instinct, is synonymous with responsibility, in this case responsibility for environmental education.

Though this book has been largely an individual effort, it would have no hope of success were it not for the educators who have been exploring the connections between education and environment for some time on their own. The correspondence and conversation I have been privileged to have with a few of those working with this approach to environmental education have encouraged me greatly. They have indicated to me that there is real hope of a constructive revolution in environmental education, a revolution that will of necessity help and be helped by the reordering of public education in general. I have tried to write the book, particularly the school and subject matter suggestions, in a way that might be useful to teachers and administrators in any given school situation, from those trapped in tradition to those taking independent routes. There is no point in my passing judgment on either of these extremes, but I would like to indicate that I think creative public education holds the most hope for both general and environmental educational reform. To support this position and perhaps to pass on a sense of encouragement to struggling public educators, I would like to quote from a short article by Dr. Forbes Bottomly, Superintendent of the Seattle school system. I am unacquainted with the success of Dr. Bottomly's efforts, but his statement in the March 1970 issue of *Washington Education* seems to me to show the possibilities open to even a problem-ridden major urban school system:

> It ought now be apparent that the interrelationship of our environmental problems with all other aspects of our lives is such that, if students are to understand the nature of these problems, the isolation wards which subject-area specialists have built around themselves will have to be torn down. In the place of departmentalization along subject lines, one could visualize a new organization emerging around the themes of health, safety and the quality of life . . .
>
> Youth must be involved at every level of planning and action if this theme is truly to unify the educational efforts.
>
> One could visualize students and teachers planning an environmental unit as a learning exercise. An environmental inventory of the school, the neighborhood around the school, the community, the town or city could be planned and carried out by the students and faculty. The results of the inventory could be analyzed and problem spots identified. Reasons for the problems could be studied with outsiders, experts and polluters asked to assist in the students' understanding of the problems . . .
>
> Why should not students and faculty of a school take a position on major matters of pollution? Student-faculty petitions to the Congress, the State Legislature, the city council, or the school-board based upon careful study and documentation, could be very effective, not only in helping students to learn how a democracy responds, but also in getting some real improvement in the environment . . . Why should not the schools confront such issues and those responsible for them?
>
> Of course, such a program would call for rather

> large-scale reorganization of the educational process. It would require the formation of interdisciplinary teams of educators, the honest involvement of youth and the development of learning-action programs . . .

Whether or not your own school district can or is willing to follow such suggestions, there is room for each of you to follow Dr. Bottomly's spirit in your own capacity as teacher, administrator, board member, or student. I hope *Teaching for Survival* proves to be a valuable aid in your efforts.

PART ONE

ENVIRONMENT AND EDUCATION

Chapter One

The Abundance of Environmental Educators

I

There is no shortage of environmental educators now, and there never has been. Only as there is a shortage of teachers in general is there a shortage of environmental educators. Throughout the history of this country, our students have been receiving about as much environmental education as one could expect. There could be no better evidence for this than the magnificent ecological crisis that has just jarred the nation into rhetorical alarm. We have taught ourselves the magic principles of a wonderland environment, we have applied those principles with an unmatched faith in their accuracy, and we have commended them to our own future generations and to the peoples of the world. Lately, we have discovered our principles belong only to our imaginations and not to the environment. Perhaps an example from my own education will show how easily and successfully environmental lessons are taught in classrooms every day.

I attended an elementary school just outside Seattle, Washington, during the early fifties. In those days I was convinced the way to train for space flight was writing and illustrating my own science fiction. I wrote stories and drew rockets at a furious rate, aiming them all at the desks of my early teachers. Somehow those good people managed to read them all and return them with glowing words of encouragement, knowing full well this meant longer stories and more rockets. Their stamina in facing these reams of pulp fiction and even more their success in teaching me the values of imagination and expression command my respect. But these same good teachers were also successfully teaching me environmental lessons that have endured for years.

Innocently, through their own ignorance and misinformation, my teachers taught me that paper would always be in infinite supply. Never was I asked to conserve and reuse my discarded mistakes, or to use both sides for a finished story. Never did I have to tolerate a lack of paper. The magic stacks of newsprint were never allowed to disappear from the shelves of the classrooms. The provision of this seemingly unlimited supply was the most effective of the lessons about paper, but supporting information filled in the environmental picture and left me little room for doubt.

We were taught that our state of Washington produced paper at a rate exceeded only by our friendly rival to the south, Oregon. And if each state produced so much and even competed to produce more than the other, it was clear our classroom would never have to worry about its supply. We knew paper was produced in pulp mills, because we occasionally were plagued by the funny smoke from the mills in Everett or Tacoma. And we were told the paper came from trees.

I could see it came from trees when I looked closely at our newsprint. In the magnificent picture space at the top of each sheet there were little flecks and fibers that looked like wood, and the teacher said they were. But knowing that paper was produced by men in nearby towns, I came to the easiest conclusion: trees gave us paper as cows gave us milk, and we produced paper as we produced milk. Vaguely, I knew the trees were cut, but that seemed the least important part of the process.

So I and all my classmates learned these three lessons: (1) There will always be paper. (2) Paper comes from trees. (3) Men produce paper. In these lessons lies an environmental education upon which a nation has been built. Never were we asked to consider any of the contradictions and paradoxes implied in the three "truths."

Indeed, their solid simplicity has helped educators teach them with ease to the present day. Were it not for lessons learned from the environment itself I am sure I would be passing on the misinformation myself.

I learned something nearer the truth about paper and trees from a bit of environment near the mouth of the Columbia River known as Long Island. A town once tried to claim the island for man but is now only a collection of skeleton pilings. I owe my introduction to the island to a teacher, but he was wiser than most. He merely showed us how to canoe to the island and how to make its acquaintance. He knew the larger lessons would be taught best by the island itself.

Long Island forms part of a large wildlife refuge in a hundred-square-mile shallow bay on the Washington coast. Geologically it is a stray from the Willapa Hills, part of the Coast Range that extends from Washington into California. It was cut off from its brothers by the waters rising since the last glaciation.

The north-facing basalt cliffs, camouflaged in mosses and ferns, darkened by shadows from great overhanging trees, and obstructed by the fallen trunks that could not hold, were in no way made for man. I have never seen or heard a dinosaur on the island, but scrambling for footholds along the base of the northern wall I am never sure that they are not eyeing me from above. In the interior of the island, the wetness, the size of the ferns, and the number of insects date the island to the coal-forming forests of the Carboniferous. But to any reader of Tolkien, the island can be nothing other than the home of the Ents, the trees towering in their wisdom.

Long Island was logged once, and most of the forest is second growth. Some of the virgin cedars, however, were too large for the early loggers and were left. There is nothing to prepare one for their size. Through the younger firs and cedars one of these elders appears first as an illusion, perhaps a stand of lesser trunks that has not yet come into focus. When the reality of the single trunk is finally undeniable, one simply stops. There is no casually passing by such age and power.

Overtowering the young forest, several of the virgin cedars had drawn lightning and been hollowed and blackened inside, their outer bark untouched by the flames. If I were to tell how the lightning left them eyes and upraised arms, looking out over the island and the bay, you would not believe me. Yet they have such heads, they do oversee the bay, and who am I to say they do not move slowly like the Ents?

Some of these gutted cedars have become the spacious quarters of local bears. Living in such elegance the bears are clearly feudal lords of the island's animals, while innumerable raccoons are condemned to a thieves' existence prowling the tideflats.

Signs of the first loggers offended us in the form of roads turned to swamps and the impossible undergrowth that follows sloppy logging. But the new forest, under the tutelage of the great cedars, appeared to have a stronghold, and we thought the island had been legislated into safety. I was impressed by the wisdom of my fellow men, who had instituted a wildlife refuge, and outlawed all but bow-and-arrow hunting, and had not rushed to provide easy access across the bay. I tried to imagine what my children's children might find when the forest was that much older, and I resolved to leave instructions for them to return.

I did not have to worry long how to leave such instructions. Soon after the island and I became acquainted, I began to see how paper and lumber are produced: the second growth is disappearing from the south end, new logging roads are following the red surveyor's flags across the island. My children's children are not likely to find anything approaching the Long Island I have known; perhaps they will find instead the efficient, calculated growth of a tree farm.

I have seen, now, how paper comes from trees: a living forest is killed; the soil it held loses its natural fertility and erodes; streams once clear are filled with sediment; the animals and plants dependent on the forest are forced into neighboring forests, if there are neighboring forests; and in a short season of logging, the members of the forest community are shown the folly of their existence. And, of course, never can the trees be allowed to grow to the irrelevant and useless size of the virgin cedars.

In this manner was my newsprint produced, in this manner it came from trees. And only if the soil is artificially maintained and forest communities are never allowed to mature, never allowed to support the animals they could, never allowed to reach the size they could; only under these conditions of environmental strife is there anything like an infinite supply. I still have trouble comprehending this environmental cost of newsprint, but I have learned, at least, that it is anything but cheap.

II

My elementary and secondary schools taught me many environmental lessons in equally innocent and effective ways. It would be neither useful nor original for me to condemn the education I received. But a beginning list of the erroneous environmental principles I learned, as well as a scheme for analyzing the educational encouragement of exploitive, insensitive environmental attitudes, may help demonstrate the nature of our problem: to change the environmental content of education, not to begin environmental education.

Environmental lessons I have learned:

> Any amount of garbage is all right, just don't litter.
>
> Population growth is good, bigger families are more fun and more people mean more friends.
>
> The Asians won't starve, as long as I eat everything on my plate and we harvest the sea.
>
> Water won't be polluted, as long as we pay "them" to build sewers.
>
> Man has always had problems, and he'll always be able to solve them through science and industry.
>
> Wildlife is a precious, but unnecessary, resource.

> Hydroelectric dams bring nothing but good: power, irrigation, recreation.
>
> Standard of living is based on annual income and purchasing power.
>
> Driving to school is approved if I am licensed, permitted by my parents, and safe.
>
> The history of man is the history of his growing mastery over nature.

And there are others I could list, as well as plenty of which I am not yet aware. Even the few listed, however, describe an environment not to be found on this good Earth.

Admittedly, more than teachers taught me about my environment. Madison Avenue is undoubtedly our most eloquent and successful educator. But the support and reinforcement the above ideas received in school was by no means insignificant. Presented without a prescribed curriculum, environmental philosophy was taught by every teacher, the school was a living laboratory, and the lack of texts on the subject only made it easier to learn. The reason for this ease of learning about the environment leads to a crucial lesson in itself.

There is no escape from environmental education, because environment *is* desks, blackboards, classmates, bulletin boards, teachers, office records, lights, windows, PA systems, grades. Each of these things is as much a part of Earth's household as any other. As each teacher approaches and interacts with every aspect of his school each day he is providing his students with a model environmental attitude. My lesson about the infinitude and cheapness of paper succeeded with hardly a word spoken: the teachers merely made sure we never ran out and never discouraged us from using as much as we wanted.

Since environment itself is unavoidable, negligence, lack of action, as even lack of comment implies that certain environmental decisions have been made. Perhaps the only other concept as sticky as "environment" is "humanity." How can we fail to project an attitude toward man by every one of our student-observed actions during the day? And perhaps we have been as dangerously inaccurate in our description of man as of environment. I believe, in fact, that the two concepts are seen as separate from one another only to the detriment and confusion of an understanding of both.

Schools may not be able to be the most forceful environmental educators; they will be hard put to command more attention than television, radio, and printed advertising. But schools need not, indeed they must not remain silent collaborators in the miseducation of the public. Both as model environments themselves, and as actual institutions making significant demands on the world environment, schools can become the focal point of a revolution in environmental understanding. They run the risk of becoming the generators of yet more environmental rhetoric. They do not run the risk of being the ultimate solution: having been asked to solve, or at least accommodate all the problems of society, schools should not even rhetorically be asked to be the solution to environmental degradation. To bring the environmental education they provide into accordance with our best environmental understanding is goal enough for schools.

A brief catalog of the most fundamental problems of environmental misunderstanding follows to complete this chapter. It is included to amplify our notion of the problem at hand and to demonstrate the dangers of teaching as usual when we are beginning to know much better.

III

It is imperative for every teacher and administrator to examine his own environmental prejudices and misinformation. Since the subtlest of everyday actions communicates about the environment as it affects the environment, a teacher cannot really know what he is teaching until he analyzes his own beliefs and habits. If we cannot discover the misconceptions we live by, then no amount of curriculum reform is going to alter the most significant content of our teaching, our actions in the school.

I have tried to catalog some general learning outcomes that provide bases for environmental misunderstanding. Achieving these outcomes is quite like falling off a log and can be done every day in the best of classrooms. We must examine our own teaching behaviors to determine how we are contributing to each learning category. Having this picture of our own teaching behavior-learning outcomes in mind, a beginning study of basic ecology, even an investigation into the nature of environment such as is provided in the next chapter, can be the means to alter environmental education to fit the environment.

Awareness

Our senses were made for the environment, there is nothing else of which they can be aware. So the problem of environmental awareness is the general problem of sensory awareness. And if anyone wonders whether or not awareness is a problem, let him visit Los Angeles, or if he lives there, let him leave.

Lack of awareness is the only explanation I can find for the Angelinos who can persist in assuring me that the smog is really not so bad on a day when I cannot help but see, smell, taste, and feel just how bad it really is. Granted they do sense the smog, but their major adaptation to it has been a lessening of sense awareness: their senses continually providing them with unpleasant reports, they have learned to ignore the information. And they have taken the imaginary environment of the media as a better, for it is surely more pleasant, indication of the way things really are: the smog alert sign says "MODERATE," the billboards all show blue sky, the travel ads are inviting people to come for the climate, and the newspaper, telling how things really are, can still be read.

A sad parallel exists in the life of most schoolrooms. Other than for the ability to read, no premium is given to acuteness of the senses. What counts is the written and spoken word. No special training is given to develop sight, hearing, smell, taste, touch. These senses are considered largely irrelevant when they do not contribute to verbal communication. And the traditional classroom is usually dull enough to inhibit much sense exploration. Since the senses provide such irrelevant information, students learn to ignore them.

The imaginary environment of the textbook, blackboard, bulletin board, overhead projector, and ditto sheet often presents all the important stimuli. Contact with real objects is at a minimum. This projected media environment is *the* center of attention in such classrooms, and success is predicated upon familiarity with it. Verbal communication is the key. The senses provide, at best, unreliable help not approved by the curriculum directors.

Through such typical practices, sensory capabilities are given no help and enough discouragement for anyone. The environment quite easily becomes the printed page, the earphone, the TV screen, the movie. They all describe the real world, which we lose the ability to sense for ourselves. (Unsettling as it is, I am afraid that lack of awareness and reliance on verbal media lie at the heart of the "success" of the Earth Day "revolution").

As long as environmental problems can be kept in the media, there will be concern and the beginnings of action. But as the focus of the media shifts, the concern and action will shift, even though the original problems are as close at hand as ever. The Angelinos may continue to go along with their smog, if it is no longer sensed through the headlines.

Insofar as any teacher fails on any day to provide an environment in which all the senses are needed, so he contributes to lack of awareness and makes toleration of environmental problems an ideal. It may sound ridiculous to ask a high-school English teacher to ensure daily that sight, touch, smell, taste, and hearing are valuable and necessary components of his classes. I suspect it sounds ridiculous only because we are already so far strayed from the awareness we once had, so adapted to rely on verbal communication. We are supposedly the most intelligent of animals, but our adaptability has taken a strange turn when we can watch the death of Los Angeles's forests from smog at a mile elevation, yet continue to live at the bottom of that deadly basin.

It is perhaps of interest to note that the Los Angeles schoolchildren, who have been feeling the smog in their lungs for years, had to be ordered to keep from poisoning themselves by exercise. Lack of awareness (of their own burning eyes and of pains in their chests) had allowed them to continue playing in the deadly gases.

Concern

Given that we and our students can become aware of environmental phenomena, what next? The ultimate problem is achieving constructive involvement in solutions to environmental problems, which will be discussed under the heading "Competence." Besides failure of competence and failure of awareness, however, I believe we educate for yet another kind of failure. I have called it concern, but the name is not important. An example from my own education may help explain.

I attended public schools near Lake Washington, a large fresh-water lake surrounded by the metropolitan growth of Seattle. This lake nearly died the premature death of Lake Erie through eutrophication, first from raw, then from treated sewage. The symptoms were the typical algae growths and an annual decline in clarity of the water.

Concerned citizens launched an effective campaign and enlisted the help of limnologists at the University of Washington. The lake was dramatically saved and is clearer now than in the early fifties. No large lake with similar problems has been treated so effectively anywhere else in the world.

I saw the sewers go in, saw the lake at its worst, felt my parents' concern, was aware that somebody was taking care of it. This all occurred during my elementary and secondary education in local public schools. Yet it never was a matter of concern in any of my classrooms. We were not encouraged to bring the situation up, our teachers acknowledged that the lake was being saved, and we all basked calmly in the assurance that something was being done.

The lesson most easily learned in those days was that pollution is not a matter of interest except ever so briefly in a Health class. If it was not worth the classroom's time, then it could not be important for success in school: it did not pay to be interested or concerned in school, even if we were aware of the problems outside. Even sensitive students can be taught to lack concern.

The environmental bandwagon now complicates matters by fostering concern without awareness: concern, in other words, focused only on the media-textbook verbalized environmental problems. Teachers boarding the bandwagon to keep their classes current run the risk of building aimless concern, even distress, in the absence of any contact with the environmental problems right under their noses.

But granting success with both awareness and concern, the difficult task of responsible involvement remains.

Competence

By competence I mean a combination of responsibility and relevance, of commitment and feeling adequate to the task. If one is aware and concerned, it is still easiest to do nothing. Some form of lack of competence is the usual excuse for inaction.

Taking a hypothetical excursion from my Lake Washington story, consider what might have happened if the schools were alive with interest and concern over the condition and treatment of the lake. I would guess that talk of solutions would begin and end with sewers: once we paid "them" to install sewers, the problem would be solved. Never would we have been asked to consider either the content or the volume of our daily generation of waste. The notion that we each were responsible for the problem, and that we each could put some limits on ourselves to help solve it would never be discussed. Nor would the heresy "Perhaps there are too many of us living around the lake" pass anyone's lips. Having paid for our sewers, we would have made sacrifice enough.

Every pollution/population problem can be directly traced to the individual: to me, to you. We have no right to feel incompetent and to distance ourselves from the problems our own demands create. Our institutional framework clouds the direct relationships that are there, but we must see through those clouds, literally, to save our lives.

Most teachers either possess the common Humanity or the Educational Psychology credits to know that students cannot be left hanging with impossible and frustrating dilemmas. Waiting, perhaps, but left hanging without hope, no. The traditional solutions to such situations are either to avoid them entirely or to end the discussion with "*They* are working on it and will find a way." Of the two, I prefer the former. At least it puts the class squarely in the field of lack of interest. The latter approach is evasive, unworthy of students' respect, often a complete lie, and promises reward for incompetence.

To educate for competence, I cannot conceive of a better way than for the teacher to be able to point to the example of his own involvement. Indeed, if the teacher is in no way involved in active solutions to environmental problems, he is a great part of the problem. More will be said of this under "Hypocrisy."

Teachers who bring snatches of their own lives into their classrooms always run risks. Those who never bring such fragments of themselves into their classrooms should not be teaching in the first place. In the case of the environment's ills, everyone is asking to see how it's done, how to clean it up. The teacher has got to begin learning himself and showing his students how. Unless such lessons of competence are learned, we will forever be ensnared in the trap that holds us now: the power company is only meeting the demands of its customers, the customers are only awaiting the company's best advice, the government is only awaiting the words of both company and customer, and all are confident that the others will soon have the solution.

Most of the remainder of this book will be given over to suggesting ways of teaching for awareness, interest, and competence. There remain two other categories of miseducation, however, which will be dealt with briefly below.

Substantive Misinformation

Return to the list on pages 7–8 for a sample of the sort of environmental misinformation that is taught. It is clear that misinformation is passed on by the misinformed, which is why the first task of any teacher committed to sound environmental education is to tend to his own education. The following story from my own brief teaching experience illustrates the complexity of the web of misinformation that is daily describing the environment.

For use in biology classes, our school had obtained a series of movies of superior quality. I was particularly impressed by one on insects. The close-up photography was impeccable, color was startlingly good, editing was smooth, the announcer was plainly a human being, even the score was less obnoxious than usual. But the lessons it taught were something else again.

Produced for schools by a major petrochemical company, the film's text told us the following: insects number more than any other class of animals (true); insects are highly evolved, very successful organisms (fine); outside of the silkworm and honeybee, very few insects are of any use to man (false); in fact, being more numerous than any other group, insects are simply man's greatest competitors for the world's food (because of whose population growth?); the most successful form of war man can wage against his "rivals" is chemical "control" on a worldwide scale (true, only in the sense that the most successful form of war itself is a nuclear holocaust). And with cutting reminiscent of the best Hollywood suspense movies, we are shown the international headquarters of the UN's war on disease and malnutrition, the company scientist in his lab, the maps of target areas, the loading of the planes, and the magnificent trails of insecticides streaming over the forests.

In order to get good close-ups of insects, it is not necessary to put up with this onslaught of disastrously misguided propaganda. The film can be shown without the sound track. Or it can be treated, with sound, as a museum piece, similar to a documentation of the arguments opposing Copernicus. One might as well be teaching that the Earth is, after all, flat, if the film is to be used simply as it comes.

The need for teachers to return to their own education and to become sensitive to the environmental implications of their own methods and of the materials they use: this need can never be emphasized enough. In terms of the environment, a misinformed teacher is a dangerous teacher. One would not want to learn first aid from one who had never studied it, but who read about it occasionally in the papers.

Hypocrisy

In the wake of the environmental revolution, curriculum guidelines are being changed, textbooks written, teaching aids prepared, all to teach the environment. New courses are being offered, old ones are covering environmental units and reading environmental chapters. Constructive as these changes may be, they are potentially disastrous if made in isolation from the school's own environment.

Teachers offering environmental courses without subjecting their own environmental attitudes to criticism are educating for hypocrisy. Small-scale examples of this were to be found in schools throughout the country on Earth Day: a lecture on resource depletion was delivered by the teacher who drives the biggest gas-eating luxury car on the market; an assembly cautioned students about the dangers of polluting natural cycles with poisonous chemicals, while outside the weeds on the athletic field were being sprayed again; a display case was filled with heart-rending pictures of our vanishing wildlands, while the oldest oak on the school grounds was cut to clear ground for the new parking lot; first-graders were taken on a litter-collecting walk, while they were still encouraged to bring their lunches wrapped in two square feet of additional paper each day.

In the self-assurance that accompanies establishing credit or time for environmental study, the danger of overlooking the real environmental problems of the school is great. If students become academic experts on ecology, yet cannot see their own ecological roles and cannot judge their own lives by the ecological principles they have learned, environmental education will not have contributed to environmental quality.

IV

"But if we tell them not to use this and not to buy that, if we tell them to limit their families, if we impose restrictions on materials in classrooms, won't we be indoctrinating rather than teaching? We can't do that!"

The teaching of environmental principles that oppose notions of property and freedom which we have held for centuries is bound to be met with the charge of indoctrination. I believe this charge can be met best with the countercharge: We *have been* indoctrinating according to one environmental view throughout the history of American education. Was it not a very successful indoctrination that taught me the "truths" listed on pages 7–8?

But the reform of environmental education should not be taken as an excuse for new indoctrination. Indoctrination should not be the method, for three reasons. In the first place, the few principles that form a sound picture of the real environment are no more controversial than Newton's laws of motion. They simply need to be taken seriously. And secondly, the science of ecology is not yet so well established that detailed, specific environmental information can be provided in most cases. For a yet more important reason indoctrination must be avoided. There is never justification for teaching students only one belief. The art of asking good questions and the science of answering them—these must be the aims of any education. Bringing our antique environmental assumptions into question, and beginning to develop the science that can provide better assumptions, these must be the aims of environmental education. Far from limiting a student's viewpoint, an awakening of environmental criticism in the classroom serves to sharpen the focus of his free inquiry into all knowledge.

It is incumbent upon all educators to face the environmental implications of their present teaching and to judge whether they have constituted an indoctrination. To open their students' inquiry into the environment, it is then incumbent upon all educators to rethink their own environmental preconceptions. It is hoped the next chapter will provide a framework from which such rethinking can be structured.

Chapter Two

Overuse and Overgrowth

I

These days it is difficult to say "Ecology . . ." and not be taken for a prophet of doom, a utopian revolutionary, or an uneasy combination of both. Much current writing on the state of the world claims that ecology has discovered Nature on her deathbed, or that ecology is the one true science/religion that will give man peace and a happy eternity. The implication of either of these assertions is that ecology, which is after all a science, has suddenly provided man the true and accurate and only conceivable understanding of the world. I want to preface my own attempt at interpreting ecological principles with a caution against such blind faith in an imperfect young science.

It is always difficult to see much beyond our own noses. Anthropologists have shown that we all hold world views through which we understand our experience and carry out our lives. According to these interpretations of the real world which continually form and reform within us, we act, think, and perceive. World views, for all practical purposes, *are* our environments. A given world view may be more or less exact or complete, may correspond better or worse with the real environment it describes. In so far as such a view closely matches reality, its holder may be considered a successful participant in reality: he is less likely to be taken by surprise, to be unaware of important phenomena. Because of the limitations of our perception and understanding, both individually and culturally, we are never in possession of a truly complete, exact awareness of the world environment.

The goal of any science is generally accepted to be the refinement of our perception and the perfection of our understanding of the world. Ecology has contributed to this effort importantly, and its lessons are desperately worth learning. But it would be a dangerous, however typical, error to assume ecology truly and completely does describe the environment. In distressing times, it is easy to believe ecology is such a perceptual panacea. The best of ecologists, however, know the haziness of their own understanding, the limitations of their research.

Though ecology is a broadly inclusive science, one can be just as ecologically narrow-minded as in any other sense. It is particularly easy to be so narrow-minded now that the word "ecology" has become heir to the most moving, confused, contradictory, and ultimately diluting connotations. We must beware the trap of labeling ourselves "ecological," while deserving only the labels "complacent" or "proud."

Teaching is not served well by a mind closed or narrowed in any direction; neither is ecology itself served by narrowness. Some of the most important concepts in environmental understanding have only been amplified by ecological research; the concepts themselves are ancient and have only needed to be taken seriously. We and our students must begin an investigation into our own environmental understanding, using ecology as a tool. No good, but much harm can come from beginning a catechism of "environmental truths", using ecology as a religion it was never intended to be.

My own attempt at understanding the environment, presented in this chapter, is not intended as a cookbook of ecology's only acceptable recipes. It is nothing other than a layman's attempt to organize his own store of knowledge. It is anything but definitive. But for me it is a useful framework, both as teacher and as participant in environment. It needs additions, it needs rebuilding constantly, and I do not advise you to accept it. Rather, measure it against your own understanding and attitudes and use it to begin analyzing your own teaching behavior.

The basic principles that follow begin to describe the world for me. Setting the current environmental situation against this description, I see two major problems for man, grossly oversimplified as "overuse" and "overgrowth." Recognizing these problems, I have tried to formulate general goals for my own teaching.

II

Area: $4\pi r^2$

The ancients knew the surface area of a sphere could be determined from its radius. A fixed radius indicates a fixed surface area. Travel on a spherical surface is unrestricted in a sense, but expansion across the surface is limited. A sphere of fixed radius is a finite object: there exist frames of reference of sufficient magnitude to make any sphere, no matter how large, small by comparison.

Since the time of the great sea explorers, man has lived with the knowledge that the Earth is spherical. For centuries refinements have been made on our measurements of Earth's radius, evenness of curvature, volume, and surface area. Recently, astronauts have seen the Earth for the globe it is and have shared this sight with millions, sending back pictures from 200,000 miles. The earlier age of sea exploration led to the age of sea colonization and sea trade. And the first implication of Earth's sphericity that man took to heart was unrestricted travel. The other corollaries to sphericity escaped him, but they remain to shape the Earth nonetheless and to affect man in their turn.

The surface area of the Earth *is* fixed at approximately 200 million square miles. Expansion across this surface *is* limited, whether it be expansion of living organisms or of particulate matter. And there most certainly exists a frame of reference within which the Earth *is* small. Men have entered this frame by circling the globe in hours, communicating across it in seconds, and viewing it from the perspective of the moon.

A good foundation for environmental understanding cannot be laid until all these implications of Earth's sphericity are taken fully into account. Astronomers may have shown us that the universe is expanding, but the Earth remains fixed in size, fixed in an order of magnitude dwarfed now by man's own flights in space.

Matter:

> "Words like 'limitless,' 'inexhaustible,' and 'boundless' . . . would not exist in a Dictionary of Nature." Georg Borgstrom, *Too Many*

A sphere of fixed radius also has a fixed volume. For this solid Earth, that means a fixed amount of matter. In terms of elements, Earth has now essentially the same composition as it had billions of years ago. Elemental matter is not changed, other than by nuclear processes going on deep in the core of the Earth and in man's reactors and bombs. The supply of elements from which both nonliving and living world were made remains constant. Astronomers have shown us that only the most infinitesimal amounts of matter ever enter the Earth from space.

The chemically combined groups of the elements, however, do not exhibit such stability. These molecules that make up the atmosphere, ocean, and crust are easily, and not always reversibly, transformed into other combinations. Thus, the chemical composition of the Earth's surface is *not* the same as it was billions of years ago, though certain forms may have remained in basic equilibrium for hundreds of millions of years under the influence of living things.

Overuse and Overgrowth

Life is dependent upon certain of these chemical combinations of Earth's matter. Life might be defined, in fact, as the continual transformation and reformation of particular compounds. The reformations, however, are not always possible. Certain transformations may result in either useless or toxic combinations for which there may be no place in the present scheme of life. Since the supply of each element is limited, toxic or useless combinations decrease the availability of material resources. Since the Earth's area is limited, toxic or useless combinations also decrease the availability of living room.

Again, our flights into space have shown us that man has achieved an order of magnitude of operations sufficient to affect significantly the chemical composition of the Earth. We need only recall the sighting of a major metropolis by its blanket of toxic smog from a Gemini spacecraft. This Earth, then, contains a finite supply of matter organized into vulnerable combinations in precious proportions.

Energy:

> "To Pardot Kynes, the planet was merely an expression of energy, a machine being driven by its sun." Frank Herbert, *Dune*

Man has known for some years that his primitive belief that the sun is the life giver is correct. Nearly all the energy powering the biological, meteorological, and to a lesser extent geochemical processes is delivered to Earth in the form of the sun's radiation. This flow of energy may be counted upon to be undiminished for millions of years, but it is a strictly limited flow, an energy ration.

Energy, though it may not be created or destroyed, may be rendered useless as it is changed from one form to another. The rule of the universe, in fact, is that concentrated, usable forms of energy are continually and irrevocably being changed to diffuse, unusable forms. This planet, as do the others, traps a tiny fraction of the sun's energy in the processes governing its atmosphere, oceans, and land. Eventually even this trapped energy, however, radiates back into space, never to power an earthly cycle again.

The evolution of living organisms on Earth created a more efficient, less easily escaped energy trap. Life, in the heat of its activity and of its decay, finally loses its grasp on the energy flow as does the inanimate Earth; but life's grasp is tighter and endures longer. The proliferation of varieties of organisms has meant the proliferation of ways to capture and recapture energy. The entire structure of life, in fact, is built on the ability of a fraction of its members to initiate the capture and storage of sun energy.

Reflecting on the status of the energy ration and on the limits of the matter supply discussed in the preceding section, we must consider the idea of production. We have seen that the forms of energy and matter may be changed, but no energy is being created, no matter constructed on this Earth. Energy is a transient visitor, continually slipping out of Earth's grasp; matter is a malleable but limited supply of clay. Production implies creation out of nothing. Though there may be room for energy and matter creation somewhere in the universe, there is none here on Earth.

We must also consider the idea of storage. Earth is a matter store, though it must be remembered that some combinations once used may not be restorable and others, once used, may become toxins or waste that are themselves unavoidably stored with us. It is only the variety of the forms of life, however, that makes Earth more than a whistle-stop for energy. It may seem as though man has increased his energy production in both agriculture and transportation by the use of petrochemicals. Really he has only opened and used the best energy stores on the planet, the plant and animal bodies that were kept from complete decomposition and oxidation under special atmospheric and geologic conditions in the Earth's past. Man has increased his consumption of this stored energy, he has gone beyond the daily sun ration of stored energy in petrochemicals; but the stores are finite, and the energy, once used, radiates out of Earth's grasp into space.

Gravity:

> "According to a recent estimate the population of the world is increasing at a rate of 123,000 per day. To remove one day's increment by... spaceship would cost about 369 billion dollars."
> Garrett Hardin, *Population, Evolution and Birth Control*

For generations man has looked to the eight other planets in this solar system as potential sources of space and materials. But the force that we've known about since Newton and depended upon since long before him, gravity, now limits any prospect of interplanetary immigration, importation, and exportation. The figures in the quotation above are more than a decade old: population now grows faster, the building and sending of a spaceship costs more.

Our population, whatever its size, is here to stay.

Our supply of matter, whether rendered useful, useless, or toxic, is here to stay and will not receive outside supplementation.

Our supply of energy is the daily sun ration, whether we use it for food, transportation, communication, or whether we allow it to be used by other life-forms, or whether we store it or not.

Gravity is going to hold Earth together, whether we try to overfill it or not. The movement of matter on the Earth, whether in living or nonliving form, will remain cyclic over the unbounded surface of the sphere. The movement of energy will remain a one-way flow, with potential eddies and backwaters, continually entering and leaving the Earth-system as radiation.

Causality:

> "We can never do merely one thing." Garrett Hardin, *Science, Conflict and Society*

The preceding sections on sphericity, matter, energy, and gravity all labor under a heavy burden of artificiality. It should be clear that matter and energy are each an expression of the other, that the finite mass of a sphere has everything to do with its gravitational pull, and that speaking of any of these phenomena as a category by itself is a questionable endeavor. As we begin to notice and to strain under such oversimplifications, we are beginning to see the world as a web.

Tracing the origins of the concept of the web of nature is a task beyond the scope of this book. I have not made a scholarly investigation into the subject, but these few observations have helped me analyze my own conception of causality. The Greek tragedians saw clearly that simple actions ramify through complex human relationships, resulting in unexpected effects and even in feedback to the initial actor. Yet the basic causal notion describing natural, rather than societal, phenomena remained linear from Aristotle to recent times. In the natural world, scientists have traditionally sought *the* cause that led to a particular effect. Few men have raised the question why nature should behave any differently than humans in their interpersonal relationships. Perhaps this is because man has been generally slow in recognizing that he and nature are, after all, one.

As our experimental devices have become sensitive enough, and particularly as we have begun researching feedback in order to design better servomechanisms, we have begun to see that the simple cause-and-effect relationship has always been a figment of our own simple imaginations. Nature is never so simple, no matter how much we have depended upon her to be. As Garrett Hardin has summarized, "We can never do merely one thing."

Migration across the planetary surface is not simply expansion of the human population. It is also depletion of other forms of life and expansion of the forms accompanying man. It is thereby alteration of the vegetation, of the soil, of the climate, and even of the expanding population itself.

Extraction of certain chemical compounds from the Earth's crust to manufacture hardware is not simply the manufacture of hardware. It is also depriving whatever organisms or processes originally depended upon the compounds. It is also depositing the compounds elsewhere, eventually, in a more or less usable or toxic state than they began, thereby affecting the organisms and processes of the deposition site. It is perhaps seeding a natural cycle that will blindly carry the compound, for better or worse, all over the globe. It is also providing for the further use of energy by the makers of the hardware and the users of the hardware, which may lead to more food, faster transportation, further extraction of additional compounds, competition for energy . . .

The use of energy is not simply the use of energy. Invariably there are by-products that may be more or less toxic or disposable, invariably there is less energy for some other use or some other organism.

These radiating effects of seemingly simple actions have been going on since the Earth began, whether we have understood them or not. And since the Earth is primarily a closed matter system, the effects have inevitably been returning to counteraffect the conditions of the initiating cause.

A corollary of the interconnectedness of nature is that no action is too small or insignificant to leave the web unaffected. Activities that we might label "doing nothing," like breathing, walking, sleeping, each send a tremor into the web, contributing either to its stability or its instability.

We have long understood that human relations are so interconnected. We are just beginning to learn in some detail that human relations reflect the nature of the environment's web. We subject ourselves blindly to the web every time we explode a nuclear device. In fact it is the dispersal of the highly detectable radioactive fallout that has most dramatically shown us the workings of the Earth's system. Finding strontium 90 in our bones, we have seen how intimately we are a part of nature. With radionuclides in our tissues, we must present the ultimate picture of folly when we still talk of cause and effect, when we still propose to do "merely one thing."

Evolution:

> "There is grandeur in this view of life, with its several powers, having been originally breathed into a few forms or into one; and that, while this planet has gone cycling on according to the fixed laws of gravity, from so simple a beginning endless forms most beautiful and most wonderful have been, and are being, evolved." Charles Darwin, *The Origin of Species*

Charles Darwin began to show man that his fellow creatures were not struck from immutable templates. Species, he said, respond to changes in their environment by themselves changing through the process of natural selection. Later studies have refined both concepts of natural selection and species. We understand now that, through the variable success of its individual members, the local species population (a group of organisms incapable of breeding with any other groups, but successfully breeding within itself) is the unit of change in evolution.

In understanding natural selection, we have begun to understand one of the major interconnections in the environmental web. Through natural selection environmental happenings leave their marks on populations of organisms. But neither Darwin, nor most of his followers, fully examined the species-environment interface. Eager to explain the history of organic forms, they postponed a full investigation of the nature of the interface, temporarily ignoring the important reciprocal to natural selection, alteration of environment.

We have long tended to think of wind and water erosion, the tides, vulcanism, and similar processes as the shaping forces of the Earth, as the environmental forces. But equally dramatic and important forces pass in the opposite direction through the species-environment interface. Living organisms cannot help but shape the environment in which they live. Coral reefs, complete microenvironments for myriads of plants and animals, are the result of the lives of the coral animals. The rich soils of grasslands would be barren were it not for the grasses themselves and the animals they support. The maintenance of nitrogen in the atmosphere is the responsibility largely of certain bacteria. Thinking back to the notion of life as a sophisticated energy trap, which is apparently not replicated on any of the other planets in the solar system, we can begin to realize just how significant the transformation of environment by life has been.

As with natural selection, the process of environmental change depends on the actions of the individual organism. As these actions are repeated throughout a locality by the members of a species population, effects become noticeable indeed. The members of a plague of locusts are doing nothing more than a single locust would do. Amplified by the plague population, what would normally go unnoticed changes an entire landscape.

If earth, air, fire, and water were the environment, or if some similar collection of inanimate things made up a backdrop for the play of life, things would be a great deal simpler. But the web of the Earth presents nothing even closely analogous to that situation. Living organisms are evolving with the inanimate world. Together they make up the environment, constantly shifting at their interface, separable only in the minds (and at the peril) of men.

Human Nature:

> "The one-eyed mollusc on the sea-bottom, feathered and luminous, is my equal in what he and I know of star clusters not yet found by the best of star-gazers." Carl Sandburg, "Timesweep"

Man has been in the process of accepting that he is an animal for centuries. Usually distracted by the effort he puts into affirming that he is also *more* or *different*, he always falls short of the acceptance. It is time we affirm that man *is* distinctive among the animals, assure ourselves of this, and then move on to the important business of accepting ourselves as, basically, animals. The intellect that we may possess in excess of other animals does not change the fundamental laws that govern our heterotrophic, consuming existence.

By being somewhat more conscious, perhaps possessed of a distinctive soul, we are not any less animal in nature. The paleoanthropological evidence of our evolution is more difficult to challenge with every new discovery: we have been shaped by the environment. The evidence that we humans interbreed successfully is far older than the science of zoology: we are a species population. We are incapable of synthesizing either matter or energy to power our own living cells: we are inextricably woven into the web of life. And our activities are obviously reshaping the Earth: we are no further from the species-environment interface than any other organism.

Man talks of conquering Nature, of overcoming her obstacles, short-cutting her laws. Every time we so assert our pride we are no different from the physicist who, at last, is sure he has built a perpetual motion machine: we haven't seen quite deeply or clearly enough into reality, we haven't waited quite long enough for all the outcomes. Look closely at every major conquest of nature, and you will find us no less subject to the interconnections and rules of the web than before. As when we claim to produce energy or material, we have simply misnamed some normal animal consumer function.

Perhaps the major difference separating us from our fellow animals is simply our capacity for worrying whether we are animals, for worrying about who we are.

III

If nothing else is clear after reading the preceding section, it should be obvious that I am neither ecologist, philosopher, nor science historian. Any of you who had expected a stimulating course in ecology must be gravely disappointed at being handed "The Earth is round, energy can neither be created nor destroyed, there exists gravity, man is an animal," and similar blockbusters. I encourage you to go to the ecologists for some of their excellent introductory works, listed in the Bibliography. But I also encourage you to look squarely at the concepts just set before you. How far do you normally carry their implications? How often do you connect their implications to the significance of your own daily behavior? In what depth do you teach them to your students?

Ecologists or not, we do participate in, and we do teach about the world. To be responsible for our own behavior and to be of value to our students, we must get as clear a picture as possible of the world. *If* ecology had all the answers, and *if* we could keep from affecting the world web while we learned about it, and *if* we could keep from imparting a world view to our students while we learned about it, then postponing a personal investigation into man's environmental relationships might be justified. But ecology does not have all the answers, we cannot keep from affecting the web, we cannot avoid teaching our students a concept of the world, and the time is now. Population, malnutrition, pollution, extinction . . . these are not simply words being sold by the media; they are realities affecting us and our students.

I have begun to approach environmental problems according to my own incomplete understanding of the world. Every teacher should begin building a similar, hopefully better and more complete world view. My own investigation has led me to categorize environmental problems under two headings: overuse and overgrowth.

IV

Overuse: subsistence needs

The energy and matter requirements of a large animal are obviously greater than those of small animals. For warm-blooded animals, the requirements are generally greater than for cold-blooded animals. The human animal is both comparatively large and warm-blooded, requiring correspondingly large amounts of food and other nutrients.

Species populations of large animals, comparable to or exceeding man in body size, tend to be considerably smaller than species populations of smaller animals. While species of insects, mollusks, and protozoa number their members in the billions, probabaly the most numerous large mammals are the species of hoofed grazers, the ungulates, who may be found numbering in the tens or hundreds of millions. Nowhere in the world does there exist a species of vertebrate comparable in size to man with a population approaching man's current 3½ billion. Rodent species or fish species may match man's billions, but no animal of human size can match him.

Knowing that Earth's energy is rationed and distributed through a complex web to the variety of living organisms, knowing that land area is limited and that important minerals are scarce, man must understand that the maintenance of basic subsistence for his present billions already puts an unbalancing strain on a finely tuned system. Many of the animals that have comparable energy and material requirements have already been eliminated or seriously reduced by man's presence: major groups of whales and larger fish; major ungulates such as the bison, and the predators whose competition has been feared beyond reason, such as the mountain lion; our fellow large primates, the chimpanzees, gorillas, and, in particular, the orangutans, whose delicate habitats have been usurped for humans.

If we did not decimate other life forms our achievement of current population size would never have been possible. We hold our species at this unprecedented size only at great expense to the rest of life, and paradoxically, at great expense to ourselves.

Overuse: artificial "needs"

On the criterion of maintenance of sheer subsistence alone there are probably too many of us now. But it is futile to argue long over that point because, of course, man does not live at the subsistence level of other animals. Perhaps a third of men far exceed the near-subsistence level at which their fellows live.

No animal of any size is capable of consuming as much of the Earth's resources as a typical resident of an affluent industrial nation. The billion or so of us who consume far beyond the necessary amounts of materials and energy succeed in multiplying the environmental effect of man many times over. For the amount of environmental room and resources we have claimed for our own, we are the equivalent of a population in the tens of billions living a subsistence existence.

The extension of our reach so far beyond what we actually need has had a number of consequences: As we near the limits of Earth's resources, the likelihood that the poor world will ever share in the wealth to which they aspire becomes less and less. As we render carbon compounds into nearly indestructible plastics, the likelihood that the carbon cycle on which all our food is dependent can be maintained becomes less and less. As we render previously "normal" elements radioactive, the likelihood that any life-forms can escape radiation poisoning and mutation becomes less and less.

Already we have begun stepping on our own toes, as is inevitable in the feedback web of the environment. Our present level of agriculture is dependent on both agricultural and transportation machinery. In order to feed ourselves at present levels, we are consuming far more than food: we are also consuming energy reserves to cultivate and distribute that food. Though it may take fewer farmers to produce an equivalent amount of food, it takes even more energy from fuel than it did originally. Our present quality of agriculture is also dependent upon artificial fertilizers, particularly in the maintenance of protein levels. The rich industrialized nations do not pull their protein out of a hat. They buy it in the fish caught by the poor nations, who need the protein for themselves but, politically, they need the money more.

The rates at which we produce changes in the Earth, through formation of useless pollutants, toxic pollutants, through domestication of food animals and crops, through extermination of competitor animals and crops, through alteration of land occupancy and use . . . these rates are unprecedented in the observable geologic history of the planet. We can be sure that we are the single most effective environmental force at least since the last glaciation. Rates of change, when normal populations are merely operating at subsistence levels, generally tend to be moderate, slow enough so that the entire life web is constantly in a state of gradual adjustment and balance. Unfortunately it takes industrial know-how to make temporary adjustments to industrial exploitation, and the other organisms have never learned the industrial way of life.

Overuse: a personal contribution

Lest we lose ourselves in the problem and become typically overwhelmed into a state of renewed negligence, allow me this digression.

My typewriter consists of many plastic parts, the keys for instance and the roller knobs. Here, then, is a collection of carbon extracted from the normal carbon cycle that is essential to plant and animal life. These plastic compounds will probably end up in the atmosphere with the destruction of the typewriter. And, as records are now beginning to show, the plastics are likely to end their atmospheric existence by entering the fat tissues of animals, and then the tissues of whomever eats the animals, and so on. Useless, potentially hazardous to the lives of the animals they will enter, these componds did not exist until a very few years ago.

The paper here also comes courtesy of the carbon cycle, but it is not such a permanent sink for the good element. It will probably find its way into the atmosphere in a useful form and may eventually find its way to the formation of another tree. But this raises another question: How long will it take? In the years that the cut forest remains bare, the richness of the soil declines and the soil itself erodes to a dangerous degree. By writing these pages I am challenging the forest to a bit of an unfair race: asking it to restore itself while temporarily impounding the resources needed for its restoration, hoping the forest grows back, but hoping to keep the paper just the same.

There is some loose change here on my table. By their ring and by the color of their edges I can see that the dimes and quarters are now sandwiched with copper, making up for missing silver. Having pulled the silver from the hills, we begin to pull the copper. But I know where we now have to go for the copper. We plan to gouge out the North Cascades and other "wild" areas. I recall the copper shortage of a few years back.

Plastics, paper, copper. I have great quantities of these substances right here before me. I seldom give them a first, let alone a second thought. In my mind I have a typewriter, paper, and some change. In reality, I have a toxic supply of formerly beneficial carbon. I have the heart of a stand of trees, possibly capable of restoring itself in my lifetime, but probably incapable of restoring the full community of plants and animals it used to support. And I have the ripped side of a mountain, ripped in order to give me a means of barter and exchange, once ripped and never to be restored. Show me another animal capable of presenting such an inventory of usurped resources, and I'll show you a human being.

But of course there is more to man's impact on the evironment than what arises from simple overpopulation. Neither is the fact that a privileged few of us are living at a level of exploitation previously unheard of in nature sufficient to explain the seriousness of our problem. There is the phenomenon of growth.

Overgrowth: consumption

Holding to the fiction that man is a species remaining at a population of 3½ billion, we find that our problems are still more complex than we have so far described. We force an even greater imbalance on the web. Our rates of consumption, which we persist in calling "production," are not constant. As if they were not already exerting a runaway force on the world, they increase by a few percent per capita annually.

The increase in consumption, in standard of living, in gross production, occurs primarily in the already developed countries. That this increase still measures as a per capita increase throughout the world's population only shows the extent to which developed countries control the world's resources. A statistical mean can show more goods and services flowing to the starving nations, along with the affluent nations, each year; in reality, the flow is almost completely diverted to the affluent.

An animal's rate of metabolism, hence his consumption of materials and energy, varies from birth to death and from season to season. Human metabolic rates peak during the infant growth spurt and then the adolescent growth spurt. But our economy is based on the constant growth in consumption, regardless of metabolic fluctuations, that meets our artificial needs, both within an individual lifetime and between generations.

I have passed through adolescence, most of my energy-consuming growth is done. Yet I certainly consume more materials and energy now than I did a few years ago: I own a car, rent a house with heating, plumbing, run electrical appliances and lights, read more printed matter, all in excess of somewhat lesser demands a few years ago. The contrast is even greater comparing my own consumption with that of my father at an equivalent age. And both my father and myself, regardless of our ages, are beset by incessant pleas to buy and use even more: I am told I should turn this typewriter in for an electric, turn my five-year-old car in for a new model, get a machine to do the dishes, get an air conditioner to cool my house. If I do not comply with these pleas, I am a grave disappointment to the national economy. Somehow we all must strive to use a little more with every passing year, we must strive to acquire a few more conveniences.

It is safe, I think, to say that had the rest of the animal world operated on such a consumption growth philosophy, there would never have been room for the merest beginnings of human evolution. Our own practice of this philosophy has already caused the termination of thousands of evolutionary paths, one for every species extinct at the hand of man. In fact, there could be no more telling sign than these extinctions: the rate of extinctions goes up with every year, quite in keeping with the increase in man's standard of living.

Overgrowth: *population*

Whether you prefer to call it an explosion, bomb, dilemma, problem, or even if you prefer to ignore it entirely, man's population growth is busy making the most elegant solutions to any other problem utterly futile. Talking of population growth, understanding it, and doing something about it are dangerously distant acts. One does not, unfortunately, lead always to the other. Once understood, the dynamics of human population tend easily to slip from one's comprehension and may never enter one's daily activities. What follows is only the briefest of reminders.

The preceding sections described man as an animal species (1) with too large a population considering his basic material and energy requirements; (2) with an unheard-of propensity to exploit far more of the Earth's resources than he truly needs; and (3) with an even more imposing habit of increasing his exploitation, per capita, each year. Distressing as man's overbearing position appears, it is not described accurately until we add the dynamics of his population. There was a point in time, perhaps as much as a few seconds in duration, when we did number exactly 3½ billion individuals. We are already well past that point, at least by a good hundred million as of this writing, certainly more by the time you read this.

In 1957 estimates gave human births in excess of deaths, net population growth, as about 125,000 per day. Even if that rate had remained constant we would have passed 3½ billion, putting that much greater stress on the Earth each day, multiplying our per capita consumption increase by a further increase in "capita": 125,000 per day works out to roughly 45 million per year: we would have gained a half billion between 1957 and 1970. Already under unprecedented pressure from the mass of consuming humans, an increase of half a billion every decade would have eventually hit the limits of environmental tolerance, especially when multiplied by the percentage increase in per capita consumption.

But we did not gain 45 million per year after 1957. During 1970 the daily increase was about 180,000: 70 million annually. And we have passed that figure now. Already the Earth is being asked to receive the equivalent of more than the current population of the United States every three years. Our population does not move from 3½ to 4½ to 5½ billion in an arithmetic progression. It is better described by the series 3½, 7, 14, 28 billion. The rate of increase which by itself threatens the stability of the environmental web is itself increasing daily.

I will not dwell on the statistics of this nightmare. I am not the writer to make the statistics speak to you. For that you should turn to the likes of Paul Ehrlich and Garrett Hardin; ideally you should dig out your almanac and play with the numbers yourself. There is just one observation on population that many have mentioned and that I would like to pass on.

The near-vertical angle of the human population curve has been observed in the statistics of some other organisms. Inevitably such a rise ends in an equally precipitous crash. Limits to the environmental carrying capacity for certain species are often easily determined. In the case of sharp population growth followed by crash, it is not the limits that are temporarily removed, but the interlocking control mechanisms, which tend to prevent such instability. The web, properly functioning, keeps moderate populations of a variety of organisms fluctuating below the limits of carrying capacity. Each population operates to curb the others; the resources are distributed rather than hoarded. Removal of a major species from the web briefly allows some other species to spurt in growth, but does not remove the limits to growth.

Man has been lifting environmental controls and removing competing species for a few hundred years. It would be difficult to convince any affluent citizen of an industrial nation that he has not removed the carrying capacity limitation. Perhaps it would not be so difficult to convince a member of the poor world who has been eating promises passed down for generations.

Unless our population growth is quickly curtailed voluntarily, a wasted world will do the job for us, indiscriminately and without conscience.

V

I hope that my attempt to summarize man's impossible situation has provoked you. If nothing else, its incompleteness should be provoking, in which case you must work out your own scheme. This was my goal in writing this section, because the words of others cannot teach you that which you have not begun to organize yourself. Do not be satisfied with my rhetoric.

Of the many good sources of environmental studies,

philosophy, and data that have recently become available, I would strongly recommend the Ehrlichs' *Population, Resources, Environment,* the National Academy of Sciences–National Research Council volume *Resources and Man,* and Georg Borgstrom's *Too Many*. These and others are listed in the Bibliography.

If there is one idea capable of summarizing our environmental status, I believe it is one that dates back at least to the Old Testament and probably earlier. As with the basic notions discussed in the beginning of this chapter, we have simply failed to take the idea seriously, we have accepted it without its deepest implications.

The idea is that we have mastery over nature, that we control this Earth. Accepting half this idea's implications, we have made the whole of it true, whether it was true when first conceived or not. But in making it true, we have brought its full implications into action. By our sheer numbers, and by our rate of consumption beyond our numbers, we have exerted our control over the Earth. We are the single most important species today, in terms of environmental effect, and we challenge many geologic and meteorologic processes as well. We do dominate the planet and increase our dominance daily.

But as any ruler is dependent upon the proper functioning of his subjects, we are no less dependent on nature than when we began. In fact the faster we have grown and the stronger we have gripped Earth's resources, the more intimately we have enmeshed ourselves in a less and less stable web. We are more vulnerable than ever to a collapse of any part of the natural system, since we depend on stretching that system to its unstable extremes.

Waking up to problems of pollution, we are only beginning to glimpse the inner workings of a planet we have been controlling blindly. The lesson that natural stability depends upon variety is bitter in our mouths when mixed with the taste of thousands of man-caused extinctions. Continuing our blind rule has only one possible outcome. Manipulating the web in incomplete knowledge may not be a much better alternative. Stabilizing our population has the potential virtue of at least winning the respect of the other members of the tattered web.

VI

The road from world population growth and resource exploitation to our classrooms, offices, or school districts may seem long and ill defined. I assure you, it shortens daily. We must begin to define it before it defines us. The main goals for educators in the age of overuse and overgrowth seem to me to be the following.

At all levels, institutions of learning contribute to overuse and overgrowth. Our first responsibility as educators is to tend to our own nests, to eliminate overuse and overgrowth in our own classrooms, buildings, and districts.

This must sound like either heresy or insanity to teachers whose schools seem always to lack the materials and resources they want. As with the world's food and minerals, we are not sharing equally in the schools. There are obviously districts and schools within districts that are truly in need of help. But for the majority of schools, I believe the problem is one of wise use rather than insufficient supply. Teachers must learn to conserve and reuse materials they now treat as expendable, no matter how they may complain about shortages.

I alternately feel reassured and shocked while writing the drafts for this book. They have all been written on otherwise wasted ditto paper, the extras and imperfects generated by one teacher's single year of dittoing. I am reassured at having found a use for them, but still shocked every time I consider their amount. The book's drafts, in fact, are accounting only for a fraction of the extras saved until the end of the year, themselves a fraction of those generated during the year. And this in a typical high school, chronically beset with a shortage of funds for new materials, and by a teacher quite aware of environmental problems.

How can we possibly educate for solutions to environmental exploitation while we ourselves remain so important a part of the problem? I fear that all the discussions about environment, all the projects, all the readings, cannot compete with the sight of this Everest of wastepaper that was somehow a part of our learning for the year. Was it really necessary?

Cutting back on our own exploitation, finding better ways to use and to reuse the resources we have, redistributing resources to share with other schools, these are all measures necessary to reduce the man-caused environmental imbalance. These measures are also necessary, however, to give meaning to any attempts we may make to offer our students an environmental education. Only if educators are demonstrably involved in finding and carrying out solutions will they have a reasonable chance of achieving the following objectives of environmental education:

The ability to perceive and to conceive of nonlinear causal relationships: We must leave Aristotle behind. We cannot afford to continue teaching the myth of simple cause and effect. We and our students must develop the awareness of causal webs operating in all areas of our environment. We must develop the vocabulary necessary to describe such causal webs. We must develop predictive abilities through gaming and experimenting with real and model webs.

The habit of speaking of the deepest implications of our world views: We must not let the ideas of sphericity, gravity, indestructibility of matter, mutability of compounds and energy, and similar ideas pass for inconsequential platitudes. Our habit of speaking of the Earth as round must become the habit of speaking of the Earth as finite. To achieve this we must develop models, games, investigations that allow sphericity, for example, to speak for itself.

The ability to sense and describe the role of any activity in shaping the environment: Developing a combination of awareness and concern as these were described in the preceding chapter, we must see how all activities and all studies are environmental. A great help in achieving this must be the development of both formal and informal interdisciplinary offerings. The mere observation that a group of seemingly unrelated teachers can communicate and jointly understand the environmental connections between their subjects can be an education in itself.

The ability to plan and carry out personal solutions to environmental problems: Here I refer back to the previous discussion of competence. We and our students must be able to consider our own behavior and to act to make that behavior ecologically sound. Crucial to the development of this ability is an understanding of the relationships between individual needs and institutional drains on the environment. There could be no better laboratory for demonstrating and investigating these relationships than the school. Equally crucial to the development of "competence" in students is the example of competence set (or not set) by the teacher.

The ability to locate and use ecological knowledge: The school must provide access to the best ecological information it can. Its environmental courses should be built around the application of ecological research to local situations. The environmental curriculum packages that are being developed should become cores of practical information for use in the school, not simply additional articles to occupy bookshelves and lockers.

The remainder of this book is a collection of suggestions of ways of reaching the above objectives. They are intended to help you get a grasp on overuse and overgrowth in your classroom, school, or district. Most of them are not pretested and validated, but hopefully they are provoking and stimulating. Within your own range of experience, perhaps a few will stimulate a web of thought and activities far beyond the imagination of this author.

In any event, I hope this collection of paper, having once been a tree, is not taken lightly. And I ask you to send it on a cycle to your friends and fellow educators so the cutting of the tree may begin to be of value.

PART TWO

THE USES OF THE SCHOOL

The categories "classroom," "school," and "district" do not begin to encompass the complexity of structures in American education. Keeping to this general framework saves us the necessity of dissecting the educational establishment in fine detail. The generality of the three categories is also intended to make the following discussion and suggestions more accessible to all educators. Hopefully both public and private schools, both large and small districts, both urban and rural classrooms will be able to use some ideas from whichever categories seem appropriate.

The categories are also general to facilitate sharing of goals and methods. When I appear to be speaking to principals, under "The School," I am speaking to teachers, superintendents, other administrators, office workers, parents, students, whomever will listen. The power hierarchies in schools certainly do not always conform to the apparent bureaucratic structure. Whoever sees that something needs to be done should begin, quietly or loudly, in whatever style is appropriate to his institution. I have watched a second-year teacher in a large high school take on the formidable task of restructuring the school's entire study-hall scheduling and format. Left to traditional channels the rescheduling could well have taken years; she accomplished it in a matter of weeks. Whatever your job description, use your foothold in the system to initiate action and discussion.

This section makes no mention of subjects or curriculum except as they are matters of school and district policy. We are dealing with philosophies, policies, and activities general to any classroom, school, or district setting. The environmental substance of the various subject areas is the topic of part three.

The suggestions may not be as specific as you expect. They do not constitute a cookbook of environmental programs. They are presented to stimulate your own thinking and design of activities relevant to your own position and, literally, environment. No step-by-step procedures from a book can be as valuable as approaches planned through your own ingenuity and experience, whatever their limitations.

I have also refrained from indicating grade levels as being particularly appropriate for specific activities. Undoubtedly there are better ages or grades for this or that activity, but I am equally positive that each activity is somehow modifiable for most levels. Any attempt to classify the suggestions according to grade level on my part would simply have resulted in a passing on of my own pre- and misconceptions about children and their teachers. Your own imaginations and the capabilities of your students will render your activities meaningful, regardless of what you take or do not take from this book. I urge you, then, to browse and to try whatever strikes your own imagination.

Finally, I would like to reiterate a caution about goals. Do not set out to "Clean up America's Environment!" Do not plan on solving all your community's environmental problems. Embarking on these voyages you are almost sure to founder in the Sea of Rhetoric. My suggestion is that you first look to yourself. Plan to build your own environmental understanding, ask your own environmental questions, and act on your own environmental ethic. Begin, then, to help your students understand, inquire, and act in order to live somewhat more ecologically sensible lives. Hopefully the great problems will be solved, but that will be a measure of the lives we and our students lead.

Chapter One

The Classroom

THE CLASSROOM AS ENVIRONMENT

As a subdivision of the world environment the classroom is as deserving as any other of receiving separate consideration. In light of the amount of time that students and teachers occupy their classrooms, these environmental boxes most certainly deserve close attention. To evaluate and explore classrooms we must keep in mind that they are both simple physical environments and purposeful, goal-oriented constructions. They may thus be evaluated both according to their basic physical nature and according to their success in attaining their specified goals.

Make An Environmental Inventory

Become acquainted with the shape and content of your classroom. There is no limit to the depth in which you can explore any environment, and these suggestions are only a beginning.

Begin with basic matter. Perhaps with the help of a custodian, determine all the materials out of which your classroom is constructed. What woods, metals, or plastics make up the walls, desks, floor? Glass, blackboards, linoleum, what are they? Any material can be considered in its molecular or elemental forms, and from these you can estimate the actual amounts and percentages of various kinds of matter that *are* your classroom. Gases, liquids, suspended dust? What are your clothes and books and papers and pencils and inks made of? Perhaps useful would be two categories, one of transient the other of permanent materials.

On another level, consider why the different forms of matter are used for the various structures in which you find them. Could they be interchanged and still make a useful classroom? Are some significantly stronger or more durable than others? What happens to those that seem to disintegrate with time? How old, in fact, are the materials surrounding you? How old are the elements composing these materials?

Move on to energy. What various forms of energy can be found? What seem to be the sources of chemical, radiant, electrical, or other forms of energy within the room? What is the energy accomplishing? What forms of matter seem particularly involved with the energy?

With a basis in matter content and energy, other levels of the classroom begin to open. What colors are to be found in the room? Examine all the materials and all the energy forms for color. Compare sensitivities and impressions about the colors. What are the light sources? How do they affect the colors?

Smell is a way of identifying matter (which you may have used to make the initial inventory). What are the smells in the room? Why do they change from day to day? With what materials and energy processes are they associated? Enlist the help of a dog. Compare our sensitivities to light and to smell, compare the vocabularies with which we describe these sensations.

What are the various surfaces of the classroom's materials? Does the same material always present the same texture? With what surfaces are we used to coming into contact? What surfaces do we avoid? Assess the variety present in the room with regard to color, smell, surface texture.

Are there sounds in the room? How does the room affect the sounds? Which sounds does the room generate?

The Classroom

Is there a variety of temperatures within the room? What materials and energies seem to be associated with particular temperatures? Are temperature changes or gradients abrupt or gradual? Does temperature seem to affect color, texture, smell, or vice versa?

Are there any things to be tasted in the classroom? Taste, more than the other senses, is restricted to use with specific intent to determine edibility. Is there any variety of tastes in the room? How easy is it to be fooled into eating an inedible material?

The environmental inventory so far is at least as much an inventory and exercise of sense abilities. This is anything but coincidental, and the opportunity should not be lost to explore where individual and environment become separate, if indeed they do.

Exploring the room, one has probably come upon animals or plants of various sorts. Do as complete a population survey of the room as possible, using microscopes if possible. Sophisticated taxonomic identification, though a good game for a biology class, need not be undertaken. Try to determine who is a permanent inhabitant, who is a transient. If your taste investigation turned up little that humans find edible, how are these other organisms surviving? Are there any predator-prey relationships or food webs discoverable among the organisms found? What factors in the environment seem to determine their distribution and success? Are there population fluctuations visible during the year?

Consider the overall shape and structure of the classroom. What parts of it are fixed, what parts movable? Just how permanent is any of it likely to be, given a long enough period of time? Are there any processes similar to erosion or deposition occurring within the room and changing its form? How does the distribution of materials affect the usable area? How do different distributions affect the "feeling" of the room?

Compared to basic sensory information, how much verbal information is being displayed or presented in the room? What forms does communication of verbal information take? Of all the material in the room, how much is used to present verbal information? Of all the energy used in the room, how much is used to present verbal information? In communication of verbal information, what are the roles played by the various senses?

Determine what attitudes affect the appearance of the classroom environment. Is there an emotional environment? How is it independent of the information environment or the physical environment? Determine what factors in the appearance of the environment affect the emotional environment.

The format of this inventory should be up to you and your students. For some, charting and graphing the results, for others, writing papers, for others, discussing the results: there is no best way other than the approach you and your students find useful and comfortable. All the questions given above need not be raised; certainly others are applicable to individual situations.

I would raise serious objections to any claim that such an inventory is too time-consuming, not relevant to a particular class, inappropriate for a particular age group, or useless. The activities of exploring the classroom, if undertaken in an unpressured manner, can easily occupy the time that is wasted in classrooms often because neither students nor teachers can be forever attending to their subject. The configuration and environment of any classroom are highly relevant to the activities of its teacher and students. No individuals, of whatever age group, can use their senses to the degree they might, and very few ever receive a real opportunity to exercise and test their sense abilities. I doubt that there is a classroom that could not in some way benefit from such an inventory, whether from discovery of actual physical limitations or from discovery of new means of communication.

Evaluate the Classroom Environment

Through analysis and evaluation, the inventory can become more than an awareness exercise: it can become the basis for a common concern.

The Classroom

Try to determine with your students what the objectives of your classroom are. "Learning" does not describe them sufficiently. The concepts should be at least as concrete as "facilitation of communication," "access to information," "experimentation with objects and processes." The discussion of just why any of you are in the classroom is always interesting and may help release a good deal of honest but pent-up opinion about the way things in general are going. To avoid such a discussion is to hide from the true environment of a classroom.

In deciding on, or at least in compiling some objectives for the classroom environment, question the items in your inventory as to their contribution toward or detraction from achieving your goals. Is access to information, for instance, better promoted by more or by less nonverbal sensory stimulation? Does the shape of the classroom contribute to full communication of all members, or does it channel communication one way? Does the classroom suffer from particular environmental problems? Does it enjoy any particular environmental benefits?

In the evaluation, if it has not come up earlier, it should become apparent just how much your bearing and policies as a teacher affect the environment of your classroom. Your behavior could not possibly be more crucial to the facilitation of communication, access to information, and possibilities for experimentation. It may seem strangely irrelevant to be talking so much of teacher policies and behavior and how these affect learning in the classroom, when we are supposedly dealing with the problems of the environment. The feeling of irrelevance should quickly wear off. We are beginning of necessity where the environment begins for our students. They spend great amounts of their time responding to and/or avoiding our presence and actions. Whether we feel like it or not, we are undoubtedly the dominant environmental force in our classrooms.

To establish the validity of concern, therefore, it is necessary to put ourselves and our actions up for discussion. Students have significant feelings and good suggestions about the conduct of classes. If they are not allowed to express these, and to express them on a regular basis, we will only be educating them to stifle their concerns. Instead we should be providing a constructive forum for the communication of concern about the classroom environment.

Experiment with the Classroom Environment

Your inventory and evaluation are bound to raise questions about better ways of proceeding. Awareness and concern, as was mentioned earlier, are of little value in the absence of competent action. The object of the evaluation, therefore, should be to plan alternate classroom styles, and these should then be tried.

Experimentation need not mean a wholesale disruption of traditional methods and arrangements. In fact true experimentation should begin modestly with the alteration of one variable, keeping other conditions constant. Pursuing and evaluating experiments on the classroom environment can become the most significant learning experience in which we engage.

Alter the configuration of the room. It is finally becoming widely recognized that the traditional row and column seating arrangement is seldom the best for facilitation of communication. Try a circle or an arc, not necessarily with you at the center. See what can be done without desks.

The easiest kinds of experiments are deprivation experiments. To determine if a material is needed or not, or if it contributes to or inhibits communication, do without it for a week. Of how much advantage *is* a blackboard, a textbook, an overhead projector, notepaper? Likewise, try to do without a given sense for some length of time. Conduct a class with all of you blind, mute, or deaf. Do without electric power. Try to discover just what your dependencies are and in what ways your classroom might be improved by the withdrawal or addition of energy or materials.

Conduct the class without benefit of plastics, glass, wood, or metals. Obviously imagination may have to be relied upon short of tearing down the classroom, but we must begin to grasp just what our material or energy needs are.

Experiment with using each of the senses sometime during each day, or with providing greater variety of stimuli for a given sense. See how much of the communication and information that passes in the class is presentable in other than printed form.

These experiments should be undertaken to improve the classroom environment's contribution to the learning processes and whatever other goals are suggested in the evaluation. Seemingly distant from the problems of environmental education, I believe they lay essential foundations for further environmental investigations. Moving beyond our consideration of the classroom as a learning environment, we may now look for expanded relationships of the classroom to the outside environment.

THE CLASSROOM AS NATURE

Besides being purposefully constructed to achieve educational objectives, a classroom is also a natural object. It is easiest to see it and speak of it as artificial, but it is in truth natural, made of the matter and energy of the Earth, constructed by one of Earth's living organisms, and somehow subject to all the natural processes of the world. When the classroom seems not to be subject to natural processes, that is the fault of our limited insight rather than a reflection of reality. Leaving educational considerations behind, then, the classroom is a useful object of study to discover how it is natural, what is happening to it, how it participates in the rest of nature, and to experiment with it as a representative part of nature.

Make an Inventory of the Classroom's Natural Relationships

The inventory of the classroom as an isolated environment could not have avoided problems of artificiality: ultimately it makes no sense to cut any one part of the environment off from any other. The atmosphere, energy, materials, position, and all other aspects of the classroom are connected to the larger environment. The connecting relationships all involve some process or collection of processes that can become the objects of this new inventory.

At some time, and preferably early and often, it is of great advantage to step outside the classroom with your students. Do this to look for qualities and relationships in the outside environment which are not readily imagined or understood. Step outside also to put the classroom box in a larger perspective and to perceive it in easier comparison to geologic, organic, or other man-made structures. A valuable line of investigation might search for an exact boundary between classroom subenvironment and outside environment (valuable because of the questions raised rather than the answers found).

An initial inquiry might proceed as follows: Certain organisms (including yourselves) that occupy the classroom are discovered to be transients, either on regular or irregular schedules. What appear to be their reasons for entering the classroom? What sort of shelter do they find? On what do they feed? If they obtain anything in the classroom, where does this finally end up when they leave? What do the organisms bring into the classroom from outside?

Having established one such connection between inside the classroom and outside, additional connections will turn up to the limits of your imaginations. For example, if the human occupants of the class appear to be the only transient organisms, one could continue in this manner: Humans breathe in the atmosphere of the classroom. The oxygen of that atmosphere, in addition to other constituents, becomes incorporated in their bloodstreams and cells. It participates in various chemical processes, eventually to be excreted or exhaled in some form other than pure oxygen. A great deal of the oxygen present in the classroom's atmosphere, then, is carried into the outside environment within the bodies of students and teachers, where it later is released in various molecular combinations.

A particularly useful combination is carbon dioxide, which may be used by photosynthetic plants in the outside environment. Depending on the region you inhabit and the amount and direction of wind currents, the carbon dioxide containing the oxygen originally picked up in your classroom may be used by aquatic algae, by cotton plants, by corn, by evergreen trees . . . Incorporated into the structure of these plants, the same oxygen may eventually end up in the fish that ate the crustacean that grazed the algae, or the clothes made from the cotton plant, or the cereal made from the corn, or the paper milled from the trees. What then is likely to be the fate of your oxygen after entering any one of these things?

With some knowledge of basic metabolism, industry, and a dash of chemistry, one can embark on a limitless game of describing the radiating connections, charting the natural web. There are many relationships beyond those mediated by living organisms. How is the classroom dependent on sunlight? A first-level answer would be that it is only minorly dependent on the sunlight entering the windows, while receiving most of its illumination artificially. But the electric power to produce the "artificial" light, where does it come from? If the power comes from a hydroelectric dam, then it is fully dependent upon the hydrologic cycle, which in turn would not function in the absence of sunlight causing evaporation and return of water to the atmosphere. If the power comes from a coal-burning electric plant, then it is dependent on energy trapped in plant material from sunlight that reached the Earth millions of years ago. And there are undoubtedly more subtle and far-reaching connections to the sun.

How is the content of the classroom atmosphere dependent upon the local environment? In urban areas it would be easy to demonstrate a direct connection as the smog content varies both in and out of the classroom. Amplifying the question to cover dependence on the regional environment, it could be demonstrated that prevailing winds bring in airs of various humidities, pressures, and temperatures, from which the classroom receives regular samples. And ultimately it would be valuable to question dependence on worldwide environment. More than likely a nuclear device has never been detonated inside your classroom, but a share of the man-caused radionuclides from the last thirty years will most certainly be found there.

How does the classroom provide habitats for various organisms, inside or out? How are these organisms changing the classroom? Are mosses or lichens gradually disengaging bricks and mortar? Are carpenter ants digesting a wall? Will the young tree that has started growing impossibly close to the wall die before its roots crack the foundations? Are any particular plants or animals flourishing on the sides shielded from the wind or sun?

Perhaps the key question that ought to guide the entire classroom-as-nature survey is: How is the classroom changing? On a daily basis, its changes are due to daily cycles of light, temperature, activity. Seasonally it takes part in weather cycles, animal and plant life cycles. Over many years it changes according to the actions of geologic cycles, eroding, settling, perhaps being shaken by an earthquake.

Any changes that seem at first unnatural, artificial, and man-induced will eventually disclose some natural explanation. A new paint job is being undertaken (to resist the eroding and cracking action of wind, rain, and sun). An air conditioner or fan is being installed (to make the sun energy of coal or streams combat the sun energy radiating through the atmosphere). The classroom seats are occupied briefly each day (to enable—whether successfully or not is another question—the occupants to learn how to use the Earth's energy and materials). There is nothing about a man-induced change that is fundamentally unnatural: it must deal with nature, and it must have ramifying effects on nature, and it really is nature acting upon itself.

Evaluate the Classroom's Participation in Nature

Having inventoried the classroom as a natural object, constructed from and participating in the natural world, it becomes possible to compare its performance in nature with other areas. The connections to nature disclosed during the inventory will most often be parts of processes and cycles. These same processes and cycles involve areas outside the classroom. For evaluation, standards of efficiency or speed might be used. In itself the choosing of standards for evaluation will raise important questions, many no doubt answerless: What should be the function of a natural area? Is one collection of organisms more valuable than another? On the time scale of Earth's existence, are any standards of comparison meaningful? Are there any clues in nature that suggest real standards do exist? Do men's actions already suggest man has decided on standards?

It would be most instructive to compare the classroom to a comparably sized area that is in a condition similar to the natural community that once stood on the classroom's site. Also instructive would be comparison to any other equivalent area in a city, whether it be part of a factory, market, street, park, or to any equivalent area on a farm, whether in a building or in a field of a particular crop. The effort of locating a community of organisms and a geologic setting similar to the original site of the classroom may be a considerable undertaking in itself. Even finding out the conditions that preceded the classroom building may require an informative search through local records or a contact with some longtime local residents.

Whatever the criteria for evaluation that are finally decided upon, there are any number of environmental parameters that can be compared or even measured. If one wishes to compare the number of organisms that are able to find sustenance and habitation within each area, one can count and estimate total populations and/or number of varieties. If there are food webs discoverable within the classroom, some observation and some natural history reading would allow the tallying of links among the organisms.

For geologic comparisons, perhaps engineers, contractors, or custodians could provide rates of decomposition and replacement of the room's building materials. Investigation of a site where a similar building has been razed would allow comparison of soil conditions prevailing beneath the classroom with those found in uncovered areas. A weather watch inside and outside the classroom could provide information on rates of wind currents, rainfall, dust settling, humidity.

An inventory of provisions for fundamental human survival needs could be taken both within the classroom and in the comparison area. An inventory could also be made of provisions for nonessential human conveniences. Communication devices in both areas, including sound, sight, smell, taste, touch—or including only those useful in verbal communication—could be compared.

If an aesthetic comparison is impossible because of lack of agreement on aesthetic values, perhaps a tabulation of the number of different stimuli present in each environment would be informative. How many different colors, sounds (within a given time), textures, tastes?

A final evaluation could be based on number and kind of learning opportunities. For what sorts of education is the classroom particularly suited? For what sorts of education is the area outside particularly suited? How many different learning devices are to be found in the classroom, how many outside? In which environment are the tests more relevant to the subject matter?

Experiment with the Classroom as a Model of Nature

Whether or not the preceding evaluation shows the classroom to be a good natural environment, the classroom can be effectively used as a model in which environmental principles may be examined. Though few classrooms can qualify as spheres, all classrooms qualify as Earth models by sharing Earth's finiteness. In some schools the effects of overcrowding are felt every day and not at all hypothetically. The lack of adequate attention given students in overcrowded classes directly parallels the lack of resources available to a species in an overcrowded environment.

If you wish to experiment with a "population explosion," there are suggestions on how to take advantage of the total school population presented in the next chapter. Within a classroom it is perhaps easiest to observe finiteness by initiating an inanimate population explosion. Chairs, for instance, borrowed from the custodian's assembly supply could be used as follows: Day 1, place one chair at back of classroom; Day 2, add one chair; Day 3, add two; Day 4, add four; and continue to double the chair population regularly, as the human population doubles regularly. The affects of such growth will go from hardly noticeable through curious to disruptive in a few days. If possible do not stop short of the disruptive stage. That unlimited growth leads to disruption is the lesson to be learned.

To demonstrate the ultimate indestructibility of matter, allow the janitorial service a month's vacation from your room. When the tide of trash becomes noticeable, perhaps students can agree on a plan to render as much waste reusable as possible . Stemming the tide of waste would be a first and very difficult goal; reversing it would be an imaginative exercise.

Experiment with Earth's energy ration by issuing each student a daily energy voucher. With this, he is limited to a specified number of statements and movements for the day. Situate a pool of fossil-fuel vouchers within reach of one corner of the class, but out of the possible range of the other students. Some form of pollution should be generated with each use of an increment of the limited fossil-fuel pool.

Gravity should manifest itself in the effects of waste accumulation, as the floor becomes the most polluted part of the room. Gravity's role in preventing an extra-Earth solution to the population problem could be explored. Have one group of students gather figures on the daily generation of people while another group gathers figures on capacity of conceivable rockets and their costs. Instead of displaying or discussing the numbers, a game can demonstrate the results: the people group is instructed to provide as many playing units (coins, cards, chips . . .) in five minutes as Earth could provide people in one minute, while the rocket group is given the task of removing as many units as rockets could according to the same time ratio. (See Hardin's *Population, Evolution, and Birth Control* or the Ehrlichs' *Population, Resources, Environment* for figures on the space exodus problem.)

The classroom is well suited to the exploration of causal webs and feedback. As a student gets up, moves across the room, and sharpens a pencil, his seemingly simple actions start waves of complicated effects. The spatial distribution in the room is altered, the sound environment is significantly affected. Visual or sound communication may be impaired for other students. The action may stimulate other students to check their own pencils and may start a series of movements across the room to the sharpener and back. A deposit of carbon is left in the sharpener which makes it necessary, eventually, to empty the accumulated residue. The student is also that much closer to having to obtain a new pencil.

The feedback to the student for his action might come in any number of forms. In some classrooms he will receive a rebuke of some sort from the teacher. He may discover his pencil is now too short to be of use to him. Upon returning to his seat, if his action has stimulated

The Classroom

others to follow suit, he may find his own verbal and visual environments impaired. In any event, he can be sure that he will not have done "merely one thing."

Communication itself can be explored as essentially nothing other than highly structured feedback. The teacher, teaching aids, and other students have come to the classroom in order to subject themselves to the causal web and to trade the feedback that is learning. In some classrooms it might be interesting to deprive either students or teacher of making a response, preventing the feedback connection for a certain length of time. The learning accomplished might then be evaluated.

The interface between organism and environment is being explored in any of the activities suggested above (and in any activities undertaken for whatever purpose at whatever time!). Additionally, it would be informative to alter the shape, size, or stimuli of the classroom in order then to analyze the effects these alterations have on students and teachers. Would any specific alterations of the environment make it uninhabitable for any of the individuals in the classroom or for all humans? Older classrooms offer rich opportunities for examining the effects of organisms on their environment in the worn floors and desks. It might be interesting to compare photographs, movies, or tapes of the classroom as it exists without human beings and as it exists with human beings. Returning to the notion of feedback, the class could also consider whether any normal activities of the dominant organisms, themselves, would affect the classroom environment so severely as to make it uncomfortable or uninhabitable for themselves.

Finally, once the classroom's connections to nature have been explored, and once it has been used as a model of nature for games and experiments, one could reconsider man. Man constructed the classroom out of nature, man receives the energy or matter of many natural cycles through his use of the classroom, man mediates the return of energy and materials to nature from the classroom. In light of these connections, of what use is it to consider the classroom as separate from nature? And if the classroom is seen to be fully a part of nature, of what use is it to consider man apart from nature?

THE CLASSROOM AS INSTITUTION

The classroom is a collection of individuals meeting together for the accomplishment of common purposes. Resources are ordered for the classroom to meet the collective demands of the group. Individual needs are summed, and the classroom mediates the fulfilling of these needs from the outside environment. This conforms to the essential nature of any of the institutions of civilization. It conforms so well, in fact, that it is useful to consider the classroom as a consuming institution and to examine the effects of its use of environmental resources.

A major obstacle to adequate understanding and to effective action regarding environmental problems is the comfortable shield of institutional consumption. We all hide behind this shield, which protects us from seeing the direct connection between our own acts and their environmental effects. Paying a water bill is distantly removed from observing the lowering of the water table, yet the act of paying has assumed the connotations of being the source of our water. In the classroom, needs and suppliers can easily be identified because of the limited number of individuals participating and the nearness to the school's ordering procedures. And because of the concreteness of some of the resources used, it is easy to experiment with efficiency of use and volume of demand. The classroom is ideal for the exploration of individual-institution-environment relationships and for the development of competence in proposing and carrying out alternate systems of usage.

Inventory the Individual Needs that the Classroom Meets

It would be useful first to set up two categories of needs: (1) survival needs, and (2) additional needs. The activity of deciding which needs fall into which category may prove to be the most informative lesson of all. It is likely to become apparent that the classroom does not provide for a great many basic survival needs. Some of these may be provided by the larger institution of the school, but some may still remain unsupplied.

Students and teachers are bound to differ on what they can get along without. An interesting line of inquiry would be to study animal and plant populations to discover if they showed similar disagreement, within a species, about what was needed. Try to reach a consensus among the class members and yourself about the needs falling within each category.

Clearly a number of needs will be for various tools, materials, and aids for learning. Ask whether any animal or plant populations set aside comparable chunks of environment solely for learning purposes. Are there any nonman-made structures or areas that supply so few basic survival requirements to their resident species populations?

There are two totals that should be derived from the inventory. Each would probably be best expressed in the form of a rate per day, though different time scales could be used. The first total: the class rate of use of each material and of each form of energy. This is the total institutional demand that the class makes for each resource. The second total: each student should arrive at a complete list of his individual daily consumption of each resource. This is his total environmental requirement per day. The figures might be more or less manageable if computed for a month's or year's duration.

Amounts of materials can easily be expressed in weights that most students can relate to known objects and to their own weights. Consumption of heating fuels is easily expressed in familiar volume units. Energy units are less commonly used and less well understood. One unit that may be meaningful to your students is the calorie. The average daily food-energy consumption for persons living in the United States is about 3,000 calories (actually 3,000 *kilo*calories, but the convention of using the word "calorie" to mean "1000 × calorie" is by far the most common usage). 2,000 calories per day would be a bare minimum for a working adult, and would be about average for a child. To convert electrical energy to calories, 1 kilowatt-hour = 860 calories; reversing the conversion, 1 calorie = 0.00116 kilowatt-hours. (Note that kilowatt-hour means "kilowatts times hours, in other words energy per hour times hours. Multiplying by hours converts the *power* measurement kilowatt to a total *energy* measurement.)

Having calculated the above totals, it might be enlightening to make subtotals of energy used for survival, and energy used other than for survival, and similarly for materials. Totaling up the inventory on class consumption is but the first step in exploring the individual-institution-environment connections.

Trace the Class's Materials and Energy to their Sources

You may already have begun something like this in locating the classroom's connections to nature. Now it is imperative to concentrate on the class as a group of individuals making collective demands on the environment. Following the principles of causal webs, an effort should be made to locate all the effects of the various processes involved in obtaining the class's resources. If any attempt to compute costs is made, do not pass over side effects that are usually not included in official economic calculations. Side benefits or side injuries are no less caused by the relevant activities simply because they may not have been intended or expected.

Direct observation of the processes and visits to the

pertinent locations should provide an active focus for the investigation. If facilities for field trips are available, then they are obviously in order. It might be less complicated, yet even more valuable, to send individual students to observe with notes or camera the various processes of supplying a classroom. Indeed, it would be difficult in the extreme to find time for a full class to explore all the ramifications of the provision of a single resource, but individual students following up individual leads could assemble a nearly complete picture.

The attempt to follow up each of the resources used in a single classroom would undoubtedly turn that class, whatever its original subject, into "Introduction to the Following Up of Resources." It would simply be impossible to do an adequate job, in a reasonable amount of time, with more than a very few kinds of materials and energy. Discuss and select one or two resources, initially, that are of interest and that seem to promise tangible results.

For example, electric power is an obvious possibility, and might be pursued in something like the following manner. Electricity makes its appearance in the room at more or less convenient wall outlets. Without tearing apart the classroom it should be demonstrable that electricity is transported by wire, generally by copper wire, and that the wire in turn must be wrapped in some sort of insulating material. Stop. Already there is the discovery that this form of energy is inextricably related to use of certain materials, notably copper and plastics or rubber. This might be called "Branch No. 1," for it leads to investigation of the mining of copper and the world's supplies of copper, both topics of great environmental interest. Also implicated is the entire synthetic plastics process, which has import both in its use of hydrocarbons derived from petrochemicals and in the problem of disposal of the durable synthetics.

Depending on how far-reaching the original classroom-as-environment inventory was, it might already be necessary to make a revision and add the estimated amount of wire and insulation needed to carry the room's electric power. With the help of custodians it should be possible to locate the connecting terminals that pass electricity in from the outside. The manufacture of the terminals and the materials involved could become Branch No. 2.

Power lines, of course, involve more materials, and estimates of just how much of which material might be obtainable from the local power company. If they are above ground, however, they may have greater interest from their effects on the environment through which they are strung. Branch No. 3 could follow both the visual and physical impact of the poles and wires, considering elements of aesthetics and safety. Again with help from the power company, information on the efficiency, the relative power leakage, might be obtainable. If the local community is at all concerned about the power lines, an extension of Branch No. 3 could involve interviews with citizens and an exploration of the problems of changing from poles to underground wiring. (And, of course, most poles were once trees—from where?)

The local power substation may take up a significant amount of land. Branch No. 4 could explore its impact on property values, the reasons for building on a particular site, perhaps the succession of a living community on its protected soil.

Before reaching a generating plant, the class may encounter a long stretch of high-tension wires. Whether these lines with their great supports travel through wilderness or tilled fields, the effects of their placement will be of interest: Branch No. 5.

When you have finally reached the source of the electricity, your problem will be deciding just what is a branch and what is main trunk. This should not be a cause of alarm, rather one of celebration: it indicates that you and your students are seeing the environment as a web.

A fossil-fuel plant raises a myriad of questions. Where did the coal or oil come from? How was it mined? How was it transported? How large are the remaining reserves? What is the content of the smoke from the combustion, and what are its effects? How is water used at the plant? How many and what sort of jobs does the plant provide?

To provide the daily quantity of electricity used in the classroom, how much must be generated at the plant, which means how much fuel consumed, smoke generated, water heated . . . ?

A hydroelectric plant raises different questions, but a myriad just the same. What are the upriver and downriver effects of the dam? What materials went into its construction? What is its expected life? Does the dam provide, in addition, irrigation? What forms of recreation did the dam make possible? What volume and velocity of water are required to provide the daily consumption of electricity in the classroom?

If you happen to trace your electricity to a nuclear plant, the questions are equally limitless. Where does the radioactive material come from? How is it mined and transported? How large are the reserves? What amount of leakage of radioactivity is tolerated at every stage of the operation? What amounts of cooling water are used, how much are they heated? What amounts of tritium and tritiated water are produced? Where do they go? How is the radioactive waste disposed of? How much material is consumed to produce the electricity used by the class, how much water heated, how much radioactive waste created . . . ?

Beginning with the wall socket in your room, there is no end to the investigation. Always be on the lookout for feedback. You may well find, for instance, that the smarting eyes and coughs to which you have become accustomed are only reactions to the smoke generated in the process of providing you with light and power. In an urban summer school, the air you are conditioning may need conditioning because of the coal-generated power you demand for your conditioner. Once through your investigation, you should be able to add a third and fourth set of totals to your original two: waste and pollutants generated per class per day, and waste and pollutants generated per student per day. The fact that the waste may be miles distant from your classroom does not in any way lessen the classroom's share in responsibility for it.

Paper is a material resource that could be followed.

Estimation of the amounts used per student per day should not be difficult to calculate or to understand. Then follow the supply chain for at least one brand of paper. The school's operating records will disclose the local source of distribution. Getting the paper from distribution center to school and from manufacturer to distribution center involves transportation and the use of energy and traffic space. The first branch of your paper investigation, then, might consider the efficiency and environmental effects of whatever types of transportation are used.

The manufacturing of paper poses a great many environmental problems. The waste products of pulp mills cause great complications in both water and air. Branch No. 2, beginning at the mill, would really require the examination of energy consumption, waste production, recycling possibilities, and efficiency. How much energy and how much wood goes into the manufacturing of the class's daily paper consumption?

Tracing the source of the mill's wood, the entire logging process comes up for investigation. Transportation of the felled trees, location of actual logging sites, cleanness of the logging technique, quality of the regenerated forest, and all the ecological effects of logging . . . these all must be counted into the provision of the class's paper supply. Branch No. 3 must finally determine how much area must be logged and how many trees must be felled to provide the class's daily paper requirement.

With paper, as with any material resource, the class is involved at the midpoint of the environmental web. Having once entered the class, the paper must be disposed of eventually. Further branches to the investigation, then, must proceed from the classroom's trash baskets back into the outer environment. How is the wastepaper collected and transported, how many man-hours does this involve? If the school does not have its own incinerator, then the question of vehicular transportation again must be answered. Where is the incineration accomplished and how much energy is required to get there? Branch No. —1 might also consider what amount of paper is actually used by the class out of the total amount that is daily discarded.

Branch No. —2 must explore the details of incineration or whatever form of elimination is employed. How much energy is used in the process? What is the content of the final discharge into the atmosphere? Where does the discharge go from there? Perhaps this is the time to consider the feasibility and efficiency of reuse processes (both within the classroom and in the garbage cycle outside).

One final interesting calculation would be the average life of the material in its paper form: in other words, how long does paper exist between manufacture at the mill and incineration at the dump? How does the paper's lifetime compare with the lifetime of the species of tree from which it was manufactured?

All the materials and energy used in the classroom can be traced in similar ways. Always the goal should be to discover the actual environmental impact, rather than the market cost, of using that resource in the classroom. Investigate chalk, ink, glass, heating fuel, fabrics, plastics, water, even the land the classroom occupies and what is involved in its use.

Do not lose sight of your original classification of needs into survival and nonsurvival categories. As much of a game as the investigation of resources can and should probably be, it is also an investigation of the involvement of a group of individuals in use of the environment. Questions of whether that use, as it becomes fully investigated, is wise or not are particularly germane.

Experiment with the Classroom's Impact on the Environment

In every classroom some decisions can be made and some actions can be taken that will help restore environmental balance. The excuses for avoiding the decisions and not taking the actions range from ignorance through negligence, tradition, despair, perhaps to vested interest. In all cases, the effect of avoiding decision and actions is an education in incompetence, and often in hypocrisy.

Once the figures have been gathered from the class's

investigation into their rate of consumption, discussions should follow on the magnitude of the class's environmental impact. With the collected data on at least some of the resources, proposals for altering or lessening the class's environmental influence should be made. Evaluating the proposals will be that much easier and more meaningful because of your quantitative equivalents established between class use and environmental effects. Notify the suppliers, transporters, and middlemen of the actions you are taking and your reasons for acting. Solicit their advice and opinions.

Paper

If you have a convention requiring the use of only one side of a page, consider dropping it, thereby cutting usage in half. Consider all the uses to which you put paper and evaluate them; perhaps some information need not be presented on paper to each individual, perhaps many activities now turned in on paper need not be. Is there any use to which used paper can be put within the classroom: wrapping, packing, lining drawers and shelves? Are there any opportunities to send used paper to a recycling plant, where it can be digested, deinked, and remade into unused paper? Can you lengthen the lifetime of the paper in any other ways? Remember to calculate trees and acreage saved, energy not used, and air and water pollutants not generated through your attempts to lessen consumption.

Electric power

Every time you would use an electric device, consider all the alternatives. Are there more efficient ways to light the room? Could class be held outside on hot days, thereby saving use of air conditioners, fans, lights, and using the energy amply supplied by the sun?

Water

In a laboratory, do you use water as wisely as you can, or is it often left running or the sink filled to wash a single test tube? In cleaning laboratory glassware or home ec dishware, what sort of soap is used; how does it rate in terms of chemical content?

Heating fuel

Are you following the best procedures for conserving fuel in all types of weather? Do you hold to certain dress restrictions that require heating or cooling that could otherwise be avoided?

Other materials

Perhaps in the context of resource utilization, a lesson about destruction of desks, tables, and other classroom targets will also have been learned. This lesson is not likely to be of much use, however, if the internal classroom environment is repressive, unstimulating, and an object of hate or scorn. One could hardly expect an individual to take positive steps to preserve an environment which he hates.

Books

Textbooks are probably the most recycled of resources in any classroom. This recycling is generally looked upon as a drawback to better learning, however, and there is always a push to acquire new ones. Does the learning in your course so heavily depend upon the text that you must have the new edition even though the others are still in usable shape? I would guess that the newer breakthroughs in knowledge would be much more strikingly and relevantly rendered through your own presentations and classroom activities. Admittedly, this is a hard one to swallow, but I would guess that the most significant thing about a textbook for a student is that it is still a book. In all but a few cases, the excitement about a new edition is shared only among teachers. For students, an expansion into new techniques of teaching and new responsibilities for them might make a much greater impact than the same old techniques and requirements garnished with a new book. Textbooks should not escape the paper resource investigation.

The most important outcome of your classroom efforts to recycle and conserve resources may not be the minuscule lowering of our gross national pollution or consumption that will ensue. You can not do merely one thing, however, and you can not proceed with such activities in a school and not expect to be noticed. The most important outcome of your efforts may well be the school's efforts, or even the community's efforts to follow in your small but definite tracks.

For your students, the most important outcome will be the beginning of an education in competence. They will have discovered some ways of behaving, individually, which when multiplied through a group have an appreciable effect on the real environment. They will also have begun to discover where they, as individuals, begin, what they need, what they can do without. This is, unfortunately, a revolutionary education in a society in which we are continually told that we need everything and anything in ever greater amounts.

THE CLASSROOM—A FINAL CAUTION

During the discussion and exploration of the classroom's environmental relationships, questions about students' and teachers' own contributions to problems outside of school are bound to arise. These questions can be taken as either personally threatening or positively constructive contributions. A teacher who has not considered his environmental role before asking his class to do so is far more likely to take such questions as damaging to his image.

If you drive to school, your students are bound to ask you why you should not be walking and not contributing to pollution and resource depletion. It is wise to be at least somewhat prepared for this type of question, but not primarily for purposes of the quick saving of face. You must begin an environmental inquiry on your own in order to be prepared to aid your students in theirs. You must begin to take personal actions to lead a more ecologically rational existence, so that you can point to a real example as your students plan their actions.

Each teacher must also be prepared to criticize his own teaching methods in order to perform the classroom environmental inventory. Our actions have disproportionately more to do with the environmental impact of our classrooms than any of our students' actions. We must also listen to our own manners of speaking, for we commonly use a host of phrases that carry loaded environmental significance. Our students may begin hearing these well before we do.

An environmental education without this self-examination and dialogue concerning personal behavior will be shorn of its interest, meaning, and ultimate impact. It is very much our behaviors that must be questioned, examined, and revised. From our various perspectives of youth and age we should engage in helping each other see the trivial gadgets and habits with which we have drained the environment. Discarding such nonessentials, we may find it easier to know the personalities they so effectively hide.

Chapter Two

The School

THE SCHOOL AS ENVIRONMENT

Most of what has been said above about the classroom is also applicable to the school. In discussing the school as an environment it is useful to keep the same distinctions in mind as were proposed for the classroom: the school is, simply, an environment; the school is also an environment intended to accomplish special purposes. But the school, from its size, arrangement, and special powers, is involved in environmental relationships that go beyond those of its component classrooms.

Evaluate the School as a Physical Environment

Proceed with an inventory and evaluation of the school building as a physical environment, a habitat. This involves listing the classroom contents as described in "The Classroom as Environment." The parent building, however, affords a much richer inventory of materials and constructions.

There is the traffic network that permits access to all rooms. The layout of this network is a dominating feature in the school environment, even if the materials used to construct it are of no special interest. Though probably a good deal less flexible than the classroom's internal arrangement, the school's blueprint is a major factor in determining the sensory milieu and the means of communication available to its inhabitants.

There may be concentrations of particular kinds of resources in the library or in resource centers. The placement of these also affects the variety of stimulation available to each student. There are special concentrations of materials in the various offices in the building. Paper will be found in great quantities in these areas, as will mechanical and electrical devices. Offices also tend to be the school's communication links with the outside environment.

At various points in the school's anatomy, water faucets bring in that precious resource, while toilets and drains provide a waste outlet. A nurse's office may contain a small store of medical supplies. Food is to be found both stored and prepared in the kitchen; special provisions for eating it are found in a cafeteria.

The school probably possesses its own heating plant and may possess an alternative electric generator for emergency use. A common waste collection station receives each classroom's and office's daily generation of garbage. Perhaps there is a schoolwide air-conditioning system complementing the heating system.

There is a certain amount of land around the building: athletic fields, parking lots, courtyards, unused land.

It should become obvious while making such an inventory that the school is a collection of materials and energy very nearly capable of satisfying most of the environmental requirements of its inhabitants. The inclusion of water and food and waste-disposal facilities are the major advances over the classroom itself. But medical supplies, communication links to the outside, provisions for vehicular access also broaden the usefulness of the school environment.

With its added resources, its connections to the outside, and its provision of space for exercise, the school building comes fairly close to being a viable dwelling place. Compared, in fact, to many dwelling structures around the world and perhaps even in the surrounding community, the school often provides more of the requirements for human habitation.

The variety of microenvironments available in the school building, from basements to eaves to playing fields to flagpoles, provides in addition habitats for other animals and plants. The inventory of coinhabitants on the school's grounds should be significant.

Of course, this provision of habitable space has been accomplished only at the expense of a great amount of raw materials. The school also makes possible and may even stimulate an even greater consumption of additional resources and production of additional wastes and pollutants. These can be explored while considering the school as an institution.

The school building, then, provides a fairly complete habitation. Perhaps it is not too early in our discussion to ask to how much use the existing school resource is put. Is its use restricted to the school day, or does the local community have opportunity to utilize its shelter and facilities? To some it may seem an impertinent question, but the daily impounding of so much space and so many valuable resources, preventing their wider use, is a profligate waste impossible for most of mankind, unheard of in nature, and unwise in the United States. Perhaps we do not put our school buildings to more efficient use in part because of what we learn in them in the first place.

Evaluate the School as an Educational Environment

In so far as the classroom is a part of nature, so is the school a part of nature. It is possible to carry on the same investigation of the school as nature as we have already done for the classroom. It is most useful, however, to consider next the school as it fulfills its prescribed educational function.

A school is instituted to provide conditions for learning. These may be summarized as facilitation of communication, access to information, provision for experimentation. All the special components of the school environment are directly aimed at these goals, or at making such aiming possible. We can evaluate these components according to achievement of the goals and also according to achievement of a knowledge of the methods of learning in general.

An early lesson that both the physical and policy environments of the school often teach is that just such a building and such policies are *essential* to learning. That they can be of great use in learning would be a more modest and more accurate representation of the learning process. It is too easy for a student who receives no contradictory information to assume that whatever happens in school, because school is for learning, is learning, including all the resource juggling, form filling, attendance taking. He learns that the best learning, if not all learning, must take place in schools.

The school environment must be presented more humbly to its students. They should learn the truer lesson that school can be a valuable environment for learning, but that man's greatest teacher has always been his original environment. The earlier that students can realize their lives do not hang on school learning, but schools can be useful places to experiment and communicate and observe, then the more successful and rational will be the operation of those schools. Students can learn in schools the value of attending to the teachings of the outside environment.

How successfully does a school environment promote communication? The most successful and satisfying form of communication is usually face to face, so the passage of myriad memos and bulletins and the frequent use of the intercom cannot be taken as evidence of communication. They may, in fact, be a comforting cover for the lack of real communication between administrators, teachers, office workers, custodians, and students. Classroom walls and departmental offices can be additional shields to the reality of other people in the school.

A major environmental hindrance to communication in most schools is their tight schedule. The absurdly short five-minute break between classes can, paradoxically, become the greatest burden for the best teachers. Their communication with students that they have stimulated cannot and should not be confined to the no-man's-land between the exit of one class and the sudden entrance of another. The pace of most schools reduces teacher-teacher and teacher-administrator dialogue to exhausted commiserations over the day's failures. What really is being gained by the cramming of so many periods into so short a schedule? The student's notion of learning and his subsequent approach to the outside environment are at stake. The crash program of the schools teaches that learning itself is a harried and swift endeavor, to the victor belongs the spoils; when, in reality, learning takes its own pace, making up in depth for whatever might conceivably be lost in coverage. To learn one principle of the natural world through actual acquaintance with the workings of the principle is to learn at least one course's worth of bolted concepts.

Is anything other than verbal communication sanctioned or suggested by the school? Students generally have their own evolving repertoire of signs and music and slaps and rumbles. Most of their schools, however, take a faintly to outright repressive stance toward any looseness of communication. Would it not be exciting, even if for only one day, to enter the school building and not see a single printed word on a poster or bulletin or blackboard? A school able to try such an experiment would be a long way toward breaking the tyranny of the written word over the life of the school. There could be no better experiment for enhancing environmental awareness. Our usual reaction to a verbally controlled visual environment is to gather all the words into our head while forgetting to notice the background. A building barren of posted words will suddenly stand out as the real structure it has been all along. The results may not be entirely pleasing, but they cannot help but be enlightening and informative.

Another more adventurous and more difficult experiment, perhaps possible only in a small school, is to set a day aside for learning in silence. Not a word should be spoken, ideally, by teacher, administrator, student, or visitor. On a first try the written word might have to be employed as a crutch, but a practiced school could develop an entire nonverbal program relying on our other means of communication.

Finally, a basic way to facilitate communication is to ask. If a school, as it begins to deal with environmental problems and to promote environmental education, perpetuates either a policy or a tradition of *not* consulting its student body about school policies and activities—then surely a most important form of communication, essential to the education of both concern and competence, will not be facilitated but inhibited. Ask your students for opinions and suggestions on any matter of school policy, whether obviously environmental or not, and a great roadblock to real environmental education will have been removed.

Does the school environment provide easy access to information? The library is probably the greatest single concentration of information in most schools. Does it function as a ready resource for students, or does it function as a bastion of precious volumes, penetrable only through use of written passes and psychological channels? The same question can be raised of departmental resource centers. Are teachers' own working libraries made accessible and useful to students, or are they kept totally out of bounds?

Assuming the accessibility of libraries and resource centers, has any attempt been made to provide access to unwritten and even entirely nonverbal information? Is there, for instance, a sound center where the audible environment can be explored? Is there some living community preserved for observation either on the school grounds, in a courtyard, or in a showcase? The school, through creative use of its common spaces and grounds, can provide a variety of types of information that, in turn, will permit a much more realistic investigation of the outside world. Again, every opportunity for exercise of sensory abilities that is overlooked and unused only contributes to our further alienation from the real environment and to our dependence on the public media.

Each teacher is a source of information. The school environment, placing teachers in personal boxes and setting apart departments, often implies that these carriers of information should be considered separate and self-contained. In reality, the information teachers provide comes into much better focus through group comparison and criticism. A less frenzied schedule, interdepartmental programs, and encouragement for teachers to share or briefly to trade classes can amplify information quality and accessibility many times over.

Does the school provide any areas for experimentation and gaming? Do school policies encourage or do they discourage an experimental attitude toward knowledge and toward learning itself? Besides being an essential part of man's environmental and social interactions, experimentation is the vital center of real learning. A psychological or policy environment that prohibits or inhibits experimentation with knowledge or with ways of learning cannot be a successful learning environment. The school building cannot help but provide a misleading aura of permanence to the learning and the knowledge it shelters. Attitudes and policies should be mustered to override this false image of man's flexible and evolving understanding of the world.

Evaluate the Environmental Policies of the School

A school need not have an office file of environmental policies to have environmental policies. As every action is an interaction with environment, so every policy has environmental implications and exerts environmental effects when enacted. In this section we are concerned with the environmental education that is delivered through the establishment of policies with environmental implications.

Consider the curriculum. Undoubtedly knowledge is most easily dealt with in small units. The traditional subject divisions allow us to treat knowledge in such units. But the environment is most definitely not divided into subunits. We see it as such due to our limitations, in part, but also due to an unnecessary enforcement of even greater academic restrictions on our education. We have dealt with the environment in subunits only at great expense to ourselves and to all living organisms.

No matter how often a teacher repeats, "Of course, all knowledge is interrelated," and no matter how many teachers offer that platitude to an individual student, twelve years' worth of exposure to pigeonholed subjects and departments teaches a lesson terribly difficult to unlearn: that reality consists of English, American history, shop skills, reading ability, chemistry, biology, mathematics, physical education . . . The most general of educations is usually made up of such specialized bits. It is no wonder that a housewife has difficulty seeing the connections between her laundry soap and the death of a lake. After all, soap is home economics, but detergents and phosphates are chemistry, the water system is health, the algae and bacteria are biology, and the lake is either geology or geography, she can't remember. To tell her that *she is the lake,* because of her effects on it and its effects on her, would be to present her with a riddle for which she is entirely unprepared.

A willy-nilly dissolution of the traditional curriculum structure might cause more problems than it would solve. Probably a more successful approach to matching education to environment is the use of interdepartmental learning teams. The subject matter, then, can be discussed and studied far more nearly as it exists in the world, whether it be a local problem, a period of history, or a political idea. Above all, schools should be cautioned to deal carefully with the presentation of any course on the environment. Categorizing such a course as social studies, science, health, or anything else, may do much more harm than the course can possibly do good. We have been living as if the interrelatedness of things were nothing but a pleasant mystical idea; the very interrelatedness of things is now showing us such behavior is suicidal.

Grades, too, carry environmental implications. Depending upon how they are used in a school, grades can become the most important form of feedback a student receives for his actions. No matter how much personal interaction has occurred during a student's education, grades can be presented and counted in such a way as to be the only significant form of evaluation, obscuring all other commentary. Twelve years of such grading is enough to teach the best of students that a simple number or letter report is the proper form of response to expect for his actions. The transfer to a diploma, a paycheck, or a traffic ticket is easily accomplished.

The environment, however, presents us with no such codified, terse evaluations of our behavior. Feedback in the environment is subtle, widespread, and long-term. If a student has never received a subtle, inclusive, and time-consuming evaluation from any of his teachers, he is that much less prepared to perceive and respond to the real environment. Grades can no doubt be used effectively, but either proclaiming them to be or acting as if they are the most effective evaluation of a student is to teach that the world is far simpler than, in truth, it is.

There is no substitute for a periodic, detailed discussion with a student about the quality of his work, the success of his learning, his reactions to teaching methods, his ideas about the course. As a student tries to construct such a discussion out of a number on a piece of paper, perhaps even received in the mail, he is trying to learn the ins and outs of a world that does not exist except on that piece of paper. If he gives up trying to decipher reality from the cryptic letter or number, we should hope that he has understood its meaninglessness; in all probability, however, he has learned that the world will accept his actions as "superior," "good," "average," "below average," or "hopeless," and will tender him similar notices throughout his life.

The content of career counseling contributes to a picture of the environment. If the only differences among industries and occupations that are discussed in counseling are in salary and prestige, then how can any be responsible for problems of mankind? It is better to make no presentations on industries and careers at all than to continue the comfortable subterfuge of mentioning only production, wages, opportunities for advancement, plant locations . . . Some businesses, as they now stand, are simply dependent upon polluting use of air, water, land. Most are still committed to increase forever the volume of their output, the amount of their sales, the number of their plants and employees, the extent of their overgrowth and overuse.

It is more than simply bad ecology to avoid mentioning the problems of an industry while discussing it as a source of jobs. If anything like a real understanding of environmental problems is reached by the consuming public and by the government, growth of industries will be curtailed and industrial roles will be redefined. In small ways this is beginning already. If the revolution in understanding gains momentum, the effects will be overwhelming. Considering careers without considering responsibility for the effects of those careers is perpetuating environmental miseducation. Considering careers without considering this possibility of sudden change in their structure is simply bad counseling.

The provision of parking space and registration to meet the growing demands of our young drivers may be a nice gesture for a high school, but it also carries an environmental lesson. It implies that driving to school is fine, as long as the student is licensed, registered, and incurs no great number of traffic violations. But is driving to school, regardless of distance and number of passengers carried, fine? By making it possible and acceptable for students to drive to school, whether they could walk the distance or not, the school is approving of a traditional but unacceptable waste of fuel and generation of pollution. All students who can conceivably walk to school should be encouraged to do so. Perhaps those who drive should have to pay a pollution parking fee according to the number of passengers they carry or the necessity of the driving itself.

This raises the question of teachers' driving: The impression given by a staff who drive to work in nothing but personal cars and from any distance is a hard one for students of any age to forget. Car pools are not just a clever idea to get the staff together, they are a beginning step toward a lessened environmental deterioration. And of course, all those teachers who can walk to school should receive every encouragement to do so.

If there still remain dress restrictions at your school, both for teachers and students, it is worth examining them for environmental implications. Clothes are, after all, for protection and comfort in spite of their use in role identification and social gratification. If, on hot days, coats and ties are still required, then environmental nonsense is being taught. The human body is admirably equipped to deal with temperature fluctuations. It will attempt to deal with them regardless of our interference, though we can make conditions such that the body cannot succeed. Light clothing is definitely an environmental improvement over tight, formal clothing on hot days. And if a choice of clothing can eliminate the use of just one fan or air conditioner, the environment will be just that much closer to being in balance. In cold weather, restrictions against the wearing of pants by girls, though they cater to some social interests, also promote environmental nonsense. (There are plenty of other reasons to eliminate or alleviate dress restrictions, but these of environmental significance should not be overlooked.)

Noise can certainly be pollution. I suppose we teachers all react first to that statement with enthusiastic approval and remember the talkers and troublemakers in class. We must be careful if we react so spontaneously. Students are learning how to communicate and are doing so in an almost entirely verbal school environment. Their talking is an exercise of the communication that is sanctioned in school. Their seemingly irrelevant and disastrous chatter is for us to listen to, not to squelch unthinkingly. It is for us to help them broaden their communicative abilities before we punish them for responding to a verbal environment with a verbal reaction. We all need most help in listening. Listen to your students well, and give them the feedback that can only come from one who does listen.

My purpose in calling attention to noise is not to give teachers an excuse for clamping down on their "little polluters." My purpose is to call attention to the school's own sanctioning of noise pollution. My target is the intercom system. If your school has one, be careful in the extreme about how it is used. If the quality of the speakers is bad, it should be used most sparingly and only after alternatives prove impossible. I have taught in a school where each morning began with a five-to-ten-minute dose of intercom announcements. Few students or teachers listened to the announcements, which most knew of through efficient grapevies already. It was most certainly noise; worst of all it was tolerated. From the toleration, the lesson was learned: pollution is a temporary nuisance and is not so hard to live with for a while. Stoic philosophy but suicidal ecology.

Undoubtedly there are schools in which the intercom system is used efficiently and even creatively as an aid to communication. Perhaps, considering time, energy, and materials, the intercom can be less of an environmental drain than any other form of schoolwide communication (to discover just how the system compares with bulletins would be an interesting and useful endeavor for a class's environmental inventory). Its problems lie not in the system itself, but in the quality of its use and, as ever, in the openness of the policy governing its use. If policy or tradition seems to permit no recourse from suffering the misuse of an annoying intercom system, then the problem of greatest importance is in the official channels of school government.

What does the policy-making structure of your school imply about the environment? If curriculum structure and content, grades, counseling service, and any of the other functions or policies of the school are never subject to meaningful student review, then the students' environment will be understood as something students are separate from, subjected to, and incapable of affecting. Whether through formal student government or informal communication, students must have an effective share of the formation and evaluation of school policy. In being aware of the school's environmental effects, students may well be far ahead of faculty and administration. Concern about environmental effects must be allowed to develop into competence in proposing and acting out solutions. Solicit student opinions and advice, and cooperate in environmental actions.

Other policies and traditions in schools are bound to have environmental importance. Some may indeed be positive and contribute to a deepened awareness and understanding of the world environment. A well-used library, for example, can be as good a model of a successful reuse cycle as can any other human institution. There is clearly a limit on the resource, books, and on the school's financial capability to acquire more of the resource. With a modicum of care, the school both uses and preserves the resource, extending both the effective range and duration of each book through the years. The school, in fact, is at least as well suited as the classroom to the modeling of natural environmental situations.

Experiment with Environmental Principles in the School

The school, with its building(s) and grounds, is an excellent laboratory and game board for the study of environmental principles. Classroom experiments like those outlined in the preceding chapter can be amplified to fit the order of magnitude of the whole school. But much more can and should be done beyond such amplification of classroom activities.

The school is particularly suited to modeling population growth and its effects. A simple classroom, without some artificial barriers raised, cannot really show crowding unless some pretext is made for dragging in people from the outside. A flexible school, however, can gradually enforce a space limitation by simple redistribution. In a school with a several-period day, for example, a day can be set aside for discussion of the population problem. First period can proceed normally, but at the end of second period each student is handed a room schedule for the day. Some variation on the following scheme can then be played: Given a school with about fifty classrooms and 1,500 students, let first period be normally scheduled with about 30 students to a classroom. For second period, eliminate ten rooms by scheduling all students who would have used them into other rooms, leaving 1,500 students in forty rooms, about 38 per room. For third period, eliminate ten more rooms in the same manner, scheduling 1,500 students into thirty rooms: about 50 to a room. Fourth period: restrict yourselves to twenty rooms, hitting a ratio of 75:1. Fifth period can be begun with the noble ambition of eliminating another ten rooms or the more realistic one of eliminating only five, giving ratios of 150:1 or 100:1 respectively. By this time something like the point should be getting across, and it is not likely that such a course could or should be followed any further. After a look at fifth period, preparations should be made for returning to a more normal distribution. In the discussions that follow it can be pointed out that the human population doubles now at a fairly regular rate, which, to model, would have required the following sequence: fifty rooms, twenty-five, twelve, six, to three for a fifth period of 500 students to a room.

A playground, gym floor, or athletic field provides room for population growth games in which the effects of choosing family size become manifest. For such games a prescribed area is set aside as the living world. Outside this area is a pool of potential people to provide the newborn and to receive the dying generation. For simplicity only one generation at a time need be left in the world, showing the population of the childbearing age group only. A more complex and realistic game requires a generation to stay in the field until the completion of two turns, resulting in a more accurate picture of the total population from the very old to the newborn. A turn can consist of some variation of the following: two people in the living world bring into the world a number of children from the potential people pool. In the simple one-generational game, the original pair now leaves the world to its new generation and joins the outside pool. In the more complex variation, the original pair remains to observe the completion of the next turn, leaving three generations present at any one time. They should join the pool, before or during the next or third turn, the bearing of their great-grandchildren. Perhaps sample rules and diagrams will help explain.

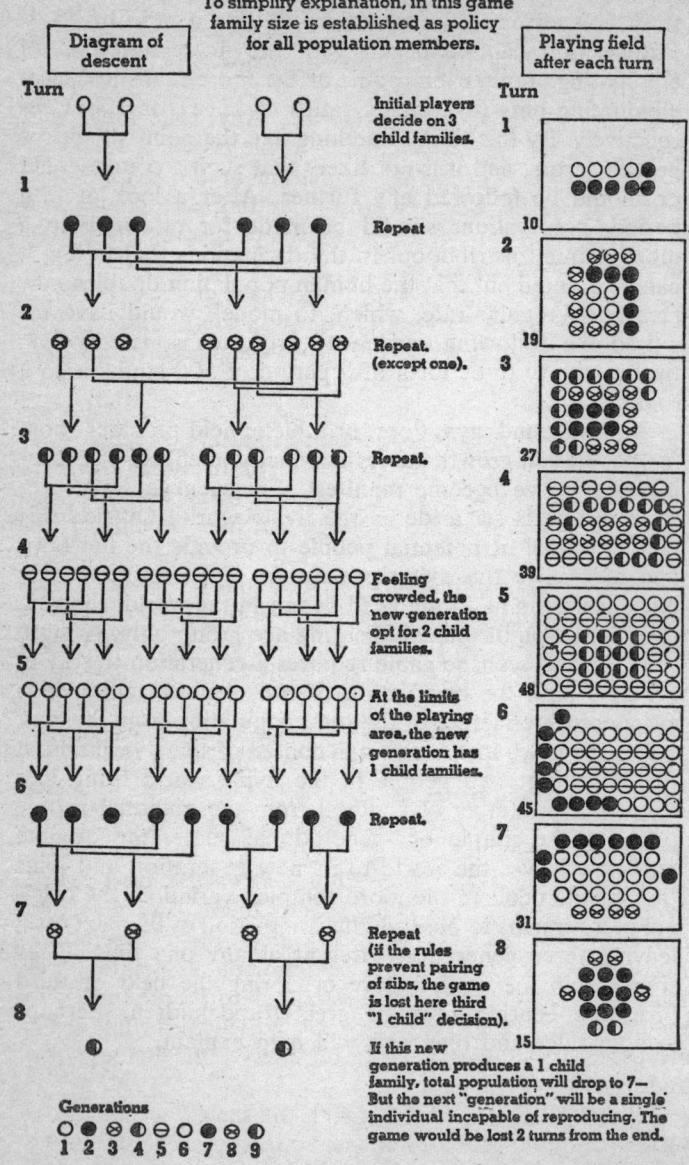

A Family-Size Game

Playing field, the "living world": Any finite area, with room surrounding for "potential people pool."

Object: To maintain a population in the living world without overcrowding and without hitting zero population.

Referee: Announces the turns, keeps records of population at completion of each turn, enforces boundary line.

Winning: The only winning will have to be relative to groups that have previously played; thus, winning will mean staying away from both over- and underpopulated extremes for a greater number of turns.

Variations: Under no circumstances should potential people and living people be allowed to talk with each other. Only within each group should communication be permitted. In the living world, talking may be prohibited either between generations, between any but family pairs, or between any players.

Members of a generation may be required to stay in the living world for three turns, or may be required to leave at the completion of their own turn.

Sample Play

The variation is that generations remain for three turns; no talking permitted between generations; family pairs chosen by counting off in twos.

Start: Choose the first four players at random to make up the first generation.

Turn 1: Family pairs are chosen from the most recent generation to enter the living world; these pairs may talk among themselves, but not with the two older generations remaining in the living world; the new pairs declare either joint or individual family-size decisions to the referee, who then oversees the entrance of new individuals; while these are entering, the oldest generation leaves the living world and reenters the pool.

Turn 2: Before continuing with the same procedure, the total population of the three generations present should be recorded by the referee, along with the number of the turn just completed; following this the new generation proceeds to pair and choose family sizes.

Turn 3: At the beginning of this turn, the new generation who chose families in turn 1 should be counted in the total population; during the choosing of turn 3, however, they should leave and reenter the pool.

Finish: The game has been lost when only one individual enters as the new generation, or when there is no room for the new generation to enter the playing area; number of turns to either of these points constitutes a score for the whole group.

Either by some variation on the above procedures or by a demonstration using only one segment of the student population, the actual growth in world population since 1650 can be modeled. Depending on the number of students to be involved and the time (an assembly, a recess period, half time on a football field), representative proportions can be established to show the magnitude and speed of population growth. The following figures may be helpful:

YEAR	RELATIVE POPULATION[a]	RELATIVE TIME INTERVAL[b]
1650	1.0	
		100
1750	1.5	
		100
1850	2.0	
		50
1900	3.0	
		30
1930	4.0	
		20
1950	5.0	
		10
1960	6.0	

[a] 1.0 = half billion.
[b] 100 = 100 years.

Taking slightly over three minutes, let us say, and starting with 10 students "in the world" representing the population of 1650, the demonstration might run something like this:

Minute 1 starts   10 students in circle (square, field, etc.)
  1650–1750: At twelve-second intervals, 1 additional student walks into circle.
Minute 2 starts   15 students
  1750–1850: Again at twelve-second intervals, 1 additional student enters.
Minute 3 starts   20 students
  1850–1900: At each of ten three-second intervals, 1 additional student enters.
                30 students
  1900–1930: At each of two nine-second intervals, 5 additional students enter.
                40 students
  1930–1950: At each of two six-second intervals, 5 additional students enter.
Minute 4 starts   50 students
  1950–1960: In six seconds, 10 more students enter.

A most fitting final remark to follow such a demonstration would mention the actual amount that world population had grown *during* the performance: in the example given above, which takes 186 seconds, world population would have grown by about 470. (Current rates of births in excess of deaths, net population increase, are 180,000/day; 7,500/hour; 125/minute; approximately 2/second.)

It is also useful to take advantage of the school as a known population and to compare its size to some interval of population growth. One can announce or display the amount of time during which an equivalent number of people are added to the world's population (emphasizing *added*, not simply born). For a school of 300, about two minutes; 1,000, about seven minutes; 3,000, twenty minutes.

It is important to remind ourselves that a scary population presentation does not help population understanding and awareness. The figures are quite threatening enough in themselves. Presenting figures or conducting population education activities in a threatening manner may well increase tension, but will dull awareness. Certainly the population problem is worthy of fear, but its solutions are to be won only through respect and responsibility.

The material resources of the world are probably best modeled by the school library. A coordinated run on library books, through planned assignments by all teachers, can effectively demonstrate the principles of the "commons." As Garrett Hardin has described these principles, the extraction of a resource by an individual benefits that individual, while it lessens the variety and amount of resources available to all individuals. As a student checks out a particular volume, his immediate needs are satisfied. The pressure on other students to check out other volumes, however, reduces each student's chances of finding any further resources. The commons will be depleted before any students have the opportunity to use more than a fraction of it.

The same principles can be demonstrated if each teacher impounds certain resources for his class by establishing an exclusive reserve shelf. Each class will be secure in its possession of one corner of the commons, but access to the library's full resources will be cut off for all. Perhaps, if a school is beset with chronic commons problems in its library without intending or planning them, a day of planned exploitation might successfully point up the problem for teachers as well as students. Following the catastrophe, planning could then be turned to ensuring smooth cycling of the library's resources.

Depending upon your school and the flexibility of both teachers and students, it may be possible to explore the effects of pollution through some controlled tests. With an intercom system, the easiest form is noise pollution: one day, certainly no more, can be tried with a constant low level of irrelevant noise piped into each room, such as a barely audible radio broadcast. Some students will no doubt be delighted to participate in such an experiment, though after a full day the pleasure should begin to wear off. Another easy form of pollution inducement, and perhaps a more instructive one, is achieved by halting janitorial service for a week. This has already been suggested as an in-classroom experiment, but it presents even more striking results on a schoolwide level.

Finally, school grounds can very effectively be used to plant and raise living communities. An on-campus terrarium in the care of students is bound to stimulate environmental questions and can lead to deeper investigations. A school in Oregon has substituted a vegetable garden for its lawns, receives organic fertilizer from the local zoo, and is carrying out an investigation into man's dependence on artificial fertilizers. An attempt can be made to reinstitute on school grounds something approaching the original community of plants and animals that lived in the area before the school was built. One can never succeed in growing and maintaining a plant or animal community without first taking many wrong turns that each carry important environmental lessons.

THE SCHOOL AS INSTITUTION

The school fits even better than the classroom the description of an institution that mediates interactions between individuals and the environment. The demands are more diverse, the collection of individuals is larger, the total environmental effects are more significant. Individual students, teachers, administrators, or interdepartmental teams can gather information on these effects. Together they can act to improve the school's environmental relationships.

Inventory the Range and Amount of the School's Environmental Demands

This is essentially the same activity described in the preceding chapter's "The Classroom as Institution" section. Again, totals and rates should be expressed both for individuals and for the entire institution. Needs should again be categorized as survival or nonsurvival. A beginning list of environmental demands might cover the following:

Area: size, shape, and nature of the school grounds before the school was built.

Shelter: amount of various types of construction materials.

Heat: volume of oil, amount of coal, kilowatt-hours of electricity.

Light: electricity and wiring materials.

Water: daily intake.

Sewage: daily ouput.

Food: daily intake.

Paper: writing, art, mechanical drawing, office, books, and all wrapping papers from cardboard boxes to envelopes.

Inks and paints: in typewriter ribbons, pens, carbons, dittos, mimeos, art and publicity uses.

Electricity: in addition to heat and light, consider food preparation, audio-visual machines, copying machines, communications.

Cleaning: ammonia, disinfectants, herbicides, pesticides.

Transportation: oils, gas, rubber, etc. (or may be considered under "The District" if controlled by district).

And undoubtedly any school makes a variety of environmental demands that can be added to the above list. It is important to include the entire school population, from principal to student, in calculating the per capita per day usages of materials and energy. An even more valuable but more difficult calculation subdivides the population into administrative, teaching, studying, and custodial groups, exploring the amounts of resources used by each. This raises some hard questions: Who uses the ditto sheets handed out as an assignment, the students doing the assignment or the teacher handing them out? Who uses the cleansers applied by the custodial staff, the custodians or those who rely on them?

The school administration can be of most help in the above inventory, making purchasing orders and other records accessible and interpretable. After the daily amount

Evaluate the Environmental Effects of the School

Examples of possible follow-up investigations of electric power usage and paper usage were presented under "The Classroom as Institution." To exemplify further the scope of such investigations let us follow, first, water, then pesticides and herbicides.

At first thought, the school's water consumption seems to be an easy calculation. Consultation with the local water authorities can secure information on the typical volume of water supplied to the school during a day. Used at sinks and taps, drinking fountains and toilets, the water is easily traced to the local water supply. Eventually some water body is reached, in the form of a stream, lake, reservoir, or ground water. It will be more or less remote and have some connection with the natural water cycle, through rain, runoff, drainage, and other processes. There will be problems with this water supply. Deforestation, cutting out competition for water by trees, also cuts out the trees' soil-holding power and permits soil erosion, lowering of the water table, and overall reduction in supply. Damming a reservoir makes water accessible, but destroys the land's original integrity and that of the living community it supported. Dams are also notoriously prone to filling with silt. Aqueducts present problematic maintenance problems, and in the end any transportation of water is depriving someplace, somehow, of its original water supply.

Unfortunately, proceeding from the school's measurable water use through the local water system shows not half the real story. For a fuller explanation of why such an investigation is far from complete, refer to chapters 6 and 7 of Georg Borgstrom's *Too Many*, listed in the Bibliography. Briefly and simplistically stated, the problem is as follows.

Water, as a medium for chemical reactions, is used in nearly every process on Earth. In the growing of one pound dry weight of edible potato, for instance, about eight hundred pounds of water must pass through the potato plant. This eight hundred pounds must be absorbed by the roots in liquid form and must be transpired into the atmosphere as water vapor. Any industrial process generating heat must be cooled, and the most common coolant is liquid water, which may be returned either as warmed liquid water or as water vapor. All the "production," transportation, and sanitation processes that support the school environment use water. The actual drinking of liquid water accounts for a tiny fraction of each person's daily water use.

The problems created by our vast water usage are especially difficult to comprehend because of a number of conditions. First, it is true that our usage does not affect significantly the total amount of H_2O on the Earth. What our usage affects is the contamination of liquid water with other substances and the overall balance between the solid, liquid, and gaseous phases of water. Second, some forms of heavy use do not disrupt the liquid water percentage, while others impound great quantities as water vapor. Many industrial uses, for instance, recycle liquid water many times over, without significantly increasing evaporation rates. Agricultural uses, however, render great amounts of liquid water into water vapor through evaporation from slow-moving irrigation ditches and transpiration through growing crops. Third, one of the most serious consequences of our overuse of water, the lowering of the water table, is usually invisible to most people. The presence of liqiud water in the soil literally makes life as we know it possible. Depletion of underground water stores is bringing us nearer and nearer to desert conditions in many areas of the globe. The problem of showing the connection of these quiet crises to our everyday living habits may be the most pressing problem in all education.

To begin to connect ourselves and our students to water usage beyond the kitchen-sink level, perhaps the only way to begin is with field observations. At a power plant, whatever kind it may be, pay as much attention to the use of water as to anything else. If the liquid water is recycled, ask to test the quality of the water as it reenters the stream or system. If the water discharges the heat of the plant through evaporation, be sure to ask for rates of discharge per quantity of electricity. Find people in the community who know about the local water table and can point to signs of its current status. Local Department of Agriculture or Geological Survey officials may be able to give you actual figures on the past and present levels of the water table and current rates of change.

When considering water use, do not fail to include all forms of material or energy use. When considering any other environmental demand, do not fail to include the nearly always significant role of water. Whenever considering the environmental impact of the school population, always figure in the per capita use of water. These totals are guaranteed to be astronomical, yet they may provide the best antidote to the feelings of individual incompetence, the feelings that no personal actions can have any significant effect on the environment. By comparison, average individual daily water consumption, as quoted by Borgstrom in 1969, was 160 gallons in the United States, compared to 60 gallons in Western Europe. A little thought can easily discover ways to cut down on our 160 gallons.

The school plays an additional role in the cycling of water which may easily go overlooked. The school's physical plant alters to varying degrees the efficiency of the rain-to-water table connection. A blacktopped parking lot does not permit absorption of water into the soil. Rainwater evaporates from the blacktop surface while running into drains. These drains may either lead the water into the soil or, more commonly, into a municipal drainage system that feeds runoff into streams or lakes. A comparison of the amount of runoff from such a covered area and the amount from an athletic field will give some idea of the school's short circuiting of the hydrologic cycle. It should then be remembered that all the covered areas on which the school depends, roads, warehouses, factories, offices, all these perform similar short circuits. Simply by collecting water on nonabsorbent surfaces, the school affects the cycling of water.

Pesticides, to keep flies out of the cafeteria, and herbicides to keep weeds out of the athletic field, allow the school to affect the world environment from seals in the Arctic to children in the classroom. The amounts of these chemicals used may be very unimpressive, but it should be remembered that they are poisons. In using them, the school is involved not only in subjecting the world to the chemicals, but in subsidizing their often hazardous manufacture and transport.

In an unknown number of cases, simply following carefully the directions and warnings on the manufacturers' dispensers is not enough caution to avoid environmental hazards. In evaluating the school's effect on the environment, identify the specific chemicals being used to destroy weeds, rats, or insects and ask their manufacturers about the testing programs that have established "safe" tolerance levels. In a great many instances proper testing has not been completed on the most commonly used chemicals. Always keep in mind that pesticides and herbicides are designed to kill organisms and that the entire science of biology is founded on the discovery that the processes of all living cells are essentially similar. Thus, the way to knock out an insect's nervous system is very often the way to knock out an *animal's* nervous system, whether insect or mammal, fish or fowl.

Sprayed chemicals seed the air with at least as great efficiency as they reach their intended targets. And the air, of course, is the unpartitioned world envelope. This explains how the chemicals used in a schoolyard in the American Midwest can end up in the fat tissue of an Arctic seal or an Antarctic penguin. Once in solution with water, either swept out of the atmosphere by rain or drained directly into groundwater through surface runoff, the chemicals enter the world-spanning water cycle. Chemicals impregnated into some substances from which they are intended to evaporate are, of course, only entering the atmosphere by a different means. It is difficult to imagine how all such evaporated chemicals are supposed to end up in the bodies of their insect targets; flies, after all, do not search the air for poisons but only take in what they happen to stumble upon.

It is interesting to speculate on the school's role in subsidizing the production of such chemicals and in transmitting them to a world that cannot escape them. Primary importance should probably be given, however, to the inhabitants of the school itself. People responsible for applying or setting out the pesticides and herbicides receive the heaviest doses. All who work or play within the vicinity of their recent application or of some evaporating dispenser are being subjected to the chemicals, either through inhalation or absorption through the skin. In the legal structure through which chemicals are approved for distribution to the public, a common principle has been that the burden of proof lies with the human body: the chemical is considered harmless until proven deadly. Until current chemicals come under adequate review and until the legal structure is changed, it seems sheer folly that schools should feel compelled to apply the same principle. Surely, at the very least, a careful review of the school's current practices is in order, searching beyond the container labels to find out just what is and what is not known about each chemical.

With individual students or teams working on particular materials or energy forms, a school can produce an impressive survey of the collective effect of its individual members on the environment. With school totals and per capita rates at hand, constructive discussions can then develop programs for effective action.

Experiment with the School's Impact on the Environment

The impact of schools on the environment is very real and very large. To say that they are institutions of consumption requires no stretch of the imagination. They exist, nominally, to make learning possible, but schools cannot accomplish their intended goal without mediating their member individuals' effects on the environment at every step in the way. Concerted action by a school population, either by revision of official policy or by voluntary individual constraint, can have an effect in improving environmental balance that is both noticeable and noteworthy.

With the students who have performed environmental inventories, with the student governing body, with all students in open meetings, plans should be laid for experiments in environmental sanity. Our society is badly in need of exemplary action toward lessening severe environmental strain, and such exemplary action, to be noticeable, must be taken by a sizable collection of individuals. The school is as good as any other institution for taking such action, and it is far better, in fact, than most. For one thing, rational environmental action contributes to the school's stated purpose, to educate about the real world.

Clean-up programs, such as were so popular on Earth Day, are valuable but are far from being the best actions that can be taken to lessen the problems of overuse. Use of less materials, recycling of materials, use of less and of cleaner forms of energy: these are the only real solutions to our greatest and most pressing pollution and exploitation problems. The public is badly in need of an example of just how effective a slight reduction in individual use can be. The school is particularly suited as an educating institution to carry out an overuse action plan, to evaluate it, and to make public the results.

Too great emphasis cannot be placed on the necessity for an action plan to be the result of cooperative effort and decision by students, faculty, administration, and food and maintenance staff. More immediate results might be obtained by any one of these groups taking action quickly on its own. Individual involvement by all concerned, however, is necessary to learn the lesson of competence. What each person now does, amplified, causes environmental imbalance; what each person can do, amplified, is the only effective balancing action. Particular groups may be best suited to obtaining specific information for evaluation of environmental impacts. Students may be able to research and visit the actual sites of processes in which the school is involved. The administration may be best able to obtain sound figures on the school's rates of use, input, and output. The information must be pooled, however, and the actions proposed must be jointly discussed and agreed upon, then jointly carried out.

The actions that your school can take obviously depend upon your current resource situation. Some schools are badly in need of some resources that other schools may be able to cut back or do without. The suggestions that follow are intended to be suggestive, not definitive.

Bulletins and memos

If these form a major means of school communication, several actions can be taken to preserve the communication while lessening the use of materials. Messages need not be double-spaced. A full sheet need not be used to carry anything but a full page of information. A deposit box can be established where once-used ditto or other paper can be collected, so that the unused side can then be used for another message, notepaper, etc.

Electricity

A simple monitoring system or an all-school responsibility can be established to ensure that room and hall lights are always off unless in actual use. Ideally, in fact, the responsibility should shift to turning the lights on, after turning them off becomes an established habit.

Food

Coordination between the food workers and students can develop a cafeteria ordering system that allows less wastage on an individual's plate and less waste margin in the cafeteria's ordering and preparation.

Recycling of materials

If there is no community collection center for cans, bottles, paper, and other recyclable materials, the school can become that center, beginning with its own significant output. Taking a first step to separate the reusable forms of garbage then gives the school a powerful voice for demanding accommodation from local industries that could accomplish the recycling.

Water

Use or time limits can be set for every sink and fountain in the school and for locker-room showers. In some schools a token form of payment for water use might begin to teach that water is by no means expendable, though it could not begin actually to pay for the environmental cost of our water use.

Pest control

In schools with pest problems, all avenues of biological control should be explored before resorting to poisons. The maintenance of school cats for rodent control or other predators for insect control might solve pest problems and teach environmental principles at the same time.

When any such activities are undertaken, follow-up evaluations are critical. Just as the full environmental costs have to be calculated in making the school's environmental inventory, now the full environmental benefits should be calculated and, whenever possible, observed. The results should be published to all school members and to the surrounding community. A reduction in the school's use of electricity, for instance, after which it is still fully capable of carrying out its educational functions, might amount to a reduction in overall energy consumption that, duplicated throughout the community, might make the new dam or nuclear plant unnecessary, or might noticeably reduce the level of air pollution from the local coal-burning generator. The establishment of a matching restraint policy, similar to matching funds policies, with other schools and with households in the community can start an environmental health plan of the greatest importance.

THE SCHOOL — ITS ULTIMATE IMPACT

Schools are human institutions, and like most such institutions most schools have a significant negative environmental impact. They drain material resources and energy, they reduce the diversity of established biological communities, they contribute to waste and pollutant accumulation. That the schools' accomplishment of educating citizens ultimately improves their environmental impact, by contributing to environmental understanding and rational environmental activity, is not always evident. In many cases, the opposite is more easily demonstrated. Students may exert an even greater environmental drain as a result of the skills and values learned in school.

Since the object of education might be stated as "ability to deal with and contribute to environments," schools have a mandate to pursue environmental rationality not so obviously given to other institutions. Schools have a duty, in fact, to follow our best understanding of the environment wherever it may lead.

Of late we have been learning some environmental lessons the hard way, by seeing how simple daily activities in the industrialized world can be suicidal. Schools can respond to this new learning by establishing environmental courses, curricula, and requirements, while not taking a second look at their own institutional operations. Such a combination of action and inaction cannot be entirely sane. It is as though a driver wary of accidents on the highway begins reading an auto safety manual while he is driving. That he is participating in reality somehow escapes him, and he feels confident studying safety principles in the abstract.

A school that becomes environmentally self-conscious, on the other hand, can become a truly educating and powerfully positive institution. A school that begins to make peace with the environment will have founded its environmental education in the reality rather than the rhetoric of the present. It will both learn more and teach more environmental lessons than are contained in any text. The ultimate impact of such an institution will be positive indeed. The feedback from a population of students that can combine knowledge with awareness, concern, and experienced competence will cause the most welcome repercussions felt throughout the living community in generations.

Chapter Three

The District

Though school district offices are certainly as much an environment for their inhabitants as are classrooms and schools for theirs, districts are of greatest impact on the environment and of greatest use to environmental education when considered as institutions. The previous sections on "The Classroom as Environment," "The Classroom as Nature," and "The School as Environment" can be read with district offices in mind. As institutions, however, districts have peculiar responsibilities and effects that merit special attention.

Evaluate the Environmental Impact of District-Controlled Usage

A transportation system is a large and important environmental influence that is often controlled by the district. At that, it is usually a far more efficient system than those employed by comparably sized industrial institutions, whose workers are most often left to fend for themselves amid a multitude of half-used private vehicles. Still, the impact of the schools' bus system is important and can almost certainly be improved upon.

An effort should be made to convince as many students as possible that they can, indeed, walk to school and will benefit thereby. The means of accomplishing this feat of propaganda must be at least as varied as the number of school districts in the nation, perhaps the number of students. I suggested this form of proexercise/antipollution campaign to some classes in a high school and received reactions ranging from "You must be kidding!" to "What a wonderful idea . . . it never occurred to me to walk!" Undoubtedly the most effective way to sell the virtues of walking would be an administration-faculty pedestrian campaign, which ideally will become a habit rather than a campaign. If just one bus can be eliminated through the growth of walking and a rerouting of the remaining buses, then a celebration can be held to show off the tangible evidence of environmental good sense in action. An encouraging thing about walking, in addition, is that he who becomes capable of a twenty-minute walk becomes capable of a twenty-five-minute walk, a thirty-minute walk, and longer walks in gradual succession. Walking to school will breed walking into town, walking to a friend's house, walking to the park, and elsewhere. Walking also contributes immeasurably to environmental awareness. Both the beauty and the ugliness that are missed on a bus ride have a much fairer chance to receive the attention they deserve.

Every effort should be made to improve the emission control capabilities of the engines in school vehicles. These efforts should be made public. If possible, the testing facilities of the school vehicle garage should be made available to administration, faculty, student, and other personnel cars. In addition, the district should bring as much public pressure as possible, in its role as a major vehicle buyer, on the bus and auto industry to manufacture environmentally cleaner engines.

The school district is also a major land purchaser and developer. Wise use and nonuse of land are at the heart of avoiding environmental collapse. If the services of a sophisticated ecological survey are too expensive for the community to employ, the district should use the best information it can obtain, namely that gathered by student teams who can inventory the biology and geology of prospective sites. On the best basis possible, the district should attempt to place and shape schools to gain from closeness to natural settings but not to destroy such settings.

The district offices are a major center for paperwork. The amount of paper used to maintain the official channels of a school district is enormous. The calculation of daily official paper use, no matter how embarrassing, will be of great value. The district offices can go far to promote environmental understanding by publicly commiting themselves to single-spaced, both sides of the page paper usage, thereby cutting their paper use by nearly 75 percent. If the initial stages of such a shift cause consternation among secretaries and correspondents, consider the consternation our practices of double spacing and single-side-only have caused the world's forest communities (and soil fertility and watersheds and on through the endless connections).

Since so much paper is used in the district offices, a sizable accumulation of reusable paper is also possible. If local paper manufacturers have not yet made reuse facilities available, the district should bring pressure to bear. The district offices may be the most reasonable collection site for the schools and the community. The environmental and psychological impact of such a recycling effort should be beneficial if not absolutely catalytic.

Evaluate the District's Environmental Policies

As is the case for the school or any other institution, official policy, whether or not it appears to deal with energy or materials, deals with the environment and exerts environmental pressures when carried out.

If a school district responds to the current environmental revolution by requiring the coverage of an environmental unit in a given course or by requiring completion of a specific course on the environment, then there is some cause for celebration but greater cause for caution. If the establishment of unit or course requirements is the only response to our environmental dilemma, great risks are being taken that threaten development of any solutions.

If the environment comes to be seen by students as yet another credit hurdle, as the property of a department, as the text of a book, those students will have lost contact with the real environment, its problems, and their roles in solving the problems. A required environmental credit or course may ultimately do much more harm than good by seasoning the environment concept with the same faint-to-strong bad taste that accompanies any requirement. A course on environmental problems or principles is best left as an elective; pressures to "take environment" should be at a minimum, so that free interest can operate.

The requirement of an in-service training unit on the environment for teachers may have similar effects, reducing environmental understanding to just another hours hurdle. The ultimate effects of such actions are usually to distance people from reality, to inhibit individual responses, and to create a tangled jargon that makes communication about the problems even more difficult.

The establishment of an Environment Day may also do more harm than good. Assembly programs must be expertly designed and executed in order even to catch students' attention. Usually a day of nonclassroom activities is valued and remembered by students mainly for the relief it provided them. If environmental problems are covered on such a day, the coverage must almost certainly be superficial, the learning insignificant. An Environment Day may easily impart a sense of action, a sense that proper solutions are underway, a sense that attendance is equivalent to competence.

The best start that any district administrator can make toward environmental education is the recognition of a school overuse problem. Actively trying to lessen the district offices' role in this overuse, he can ask the help of administrators, teachers, and students to study and act to alleviate the problem. Dealing in specifics, he does not have to suffer the unmanageability of environmental jargon. Studying to find a solution, he is promoting the learning of environmental principles. Acting on the principles, he is accomplishing effective environmental reform and is demonstrating that the environment, its ills and complications included, is real and accessible.

One particularly important role that the district can play is in distribution of resources. In many districts there are the have and the have-not schools, mirroring the imbalances in resource use among men, and between men and the rest of the living world. As schools find that they can cut back on their use of various materials, perhaps the money or the materials themselves can aid those schools that really are in need of help.

Evaluate the District's Dependence on the Overgrowth Cycle

This must ultimately be the most difficult problem for the schools as well as the rest of the nation to deal with. In *The American School,* Patricia Cayo Sexton states flatly, "The future of the schools depends, then, upon . . . the ability of the American economy to stabilize at high growth rates . . ." This statement is indisputably true, but perhaps not in the sense originally intended. Because of environmental limitations, such as those that operate for any other living organism, man's future is going to depend upon the *in*ability of his economy to stabilize at high growth rates, and upon his success in adjusting to this limitation.

Just how caught up in the overgrowth spiral are schools? In examining the tax base of the local community, just how dependent are schools on the taxes derived from industries whose avowed aim is growth and expansion? And in order to use more resources and to hire more teachers, just how actively has the school district tried to promote local development and growth?

Overcrowded schools are prime examples of the debilitating stresses and strains caused by population growth. Unfortunately first recourse has usually been sought in economic overgrowth to alleviate those stresses and strains. On an expanding planet, such policies would make the best of sense, but on Earth they are the ultimate folly.

A reordering of the nation's economy is sure to come as our environmental limits are met. The wisdom and success of this reordering will depend upon how soon before growth must stop we begin actively to slow the economic pace. In the reordering that will ensue, the system of support for schools will have to undergo major revisions.

For me to plot this reordering would be amusing at best. But I believe I can see a first step for the schools that can best be taken at the district level. That is, simply stop promoting overgrowth. Dependence on it will not be easily broken, but at least active promotion can be curtailed. Whatever efforts the schools can make to decrease their own overuse will help support such a policy of abstention from overgrowth promotion. In taking such actions, the district can begin to bring the community together to discuss the economic problems that are imminent and to develop programs and solutions. The schools can thus help ease the transition by opening the discussion early (early compared to other institutions, not early in view of our nearness to environmental limits).

PART THREE

THE SUBJECT MATTERS

No subject can be studied in isolation from the environment. Each subject has some history of interaction with the environment and presents some image of the environment. In studying a subject it is well for us to remember the words of John Muir: "When we try to pick out anything by itself, we find it hitched to everything else in the universe." A corollary to Garrett Hardin's statement on the interconnectedness of things (p. 26) is "We can never *study* merely one thing."

The fact that environment is interwoven into every subject matter does not mean that every class must become an ecology class overnight. Ecology is a developing science that still deserves and benefits from separate attention in building and criticizing its body of knowldge. But certain principles that ecology has discovered or upon which ecology has thrown light have very great implications for all bodies of man's knowledge. Locating and observing the actions of these principles from the various subject perspectives can deepen understanding of subjects and sharpen their perspectives.

The following chapters are not written with the intent of showing how to produce instant ecology, or how to jump on the environmental bandwagon to make classes "current." They are written, rather, to suggest the working of ecological principles within the various subjects and to suggest how certain activities can promote deeper study of both subject and environment.

The classification of subjects in this book as observers, interpreters, and users is not intended to be definitive. Its flaws are obvious: every subject observes, interprets, and uses the environment. I have tried, however, to decide where the major environmental emphasis lies for each subject. I have also purposefully avoided traditional department boundaries. Divisions such as social science, natural science, humanities, and vocations seem to me to present an erroneous picture of environmental relationships. The classifications presented here result from an attempt to find environmentally meaningful alternatives to the traditional divisions.

Chapter One

The Observers

Through the observers, man seeks to understand the workings of the environment. One of the observer groups, the Earth sciences, has become heir to a name that should describe them all. All these subjects are Earth sciences, whether they have traditionally been considered sciences or humanities. They are together involved in observing and recording qualitative and quantitative information about the Earth environment. To paraphrase Max Nicholson, as they study "the tale of man's Earth," they are studying "the mirror image of Earth's man"; as they study man, they are studying a manifestation of the Earth.

The findings of the observers are intended to be useful to man, to allow him more successful use of his environment. The observers' environmental understanding is applied in new forms of environmental use. Seldom are such applications made by the users, however, without the intervention of values arrived at by the interpreters. The observers have a great responsibility to maintain close communication with the interpreters and the users and to continue to observe the effects of the application of their knowledge. If values conflict with environmental principles, for instance, the observers have an obligation to speak out and to participate in the building of new values.

The study of the observer subjects in school affords

opportunities for practice of environmental awareness, for interaction with environment through experimentation, and for evaluation of the effects of application of the observers' findings by society. Interdisciplinary study within the observers can promote an even deeper understanding of the environment. The development of fringe subjects in the observers has shown the necessity of treating the environment as a continuum. Increasingly these fields are turning out important new information, as in biochemistry, geophysics, socioeconomics, historical psychology. This interdisciplinary coordination must become the rule rather than the exception in education.

Anthropology

I once presented a summer course on evolutionary anthropology to a group of high-school sophomores, relying for much of our material on the leaflet versions of the American Anthropology Association's planned secondary anthropology course. One fascinating activity, suggested by the AAA and carried out in our course, is the reconstruction of Bushman life from the mapped findings of an archaeological dig. With maps, diagrams, and a few sample artifacts, students are given the problem of elucidating the habits of the Kalahari people. A coordinate reading is entitled "Grand Central Station" and poses the question of what future archaeologists of the North American continent might find if they uncovered the remains of New York City.

We looked around our own school grounds and tried to imagine how we would appear from the perspective of a few millennia or longer. A point beautifully and quietly made, which we took for the main point of the lesson, was the limitation on accuracy of any scientific investigation, and of archaeological and paleontological investigations in particular. I now regret that we left it at that, and I hope that the experience was vivid enough for my students so that they have returned to it in their minds as I have in mine.

Surely a valuable, if indeed not the most valuable teaching of archaeology must be that man and all his works are one with Earth. We eventually become passive components of rock formations, river deltas, and ocean bottoms, returning to the matter and processes that gave us our beginnings. Our tacit assumption that modern buildings are capable of withstanding the elements is no more convincing than was the similar assumption of the Egyptians. I wish that our class had tarried a little longer with archaeology so that the insight of oneness with environment might have occurred to us. It is a lesson difficult to verbalize in any creative or convincing way, but the sight of a Pleistocene flint next to a beer can in the same stream bed can convey it in unforgettable imagery.

The study of man is the study of man's environmental interactions. Archaeology tends to reconstruct those interactions from remains that have begun their gradual return to inhuman existence. Physical anthropology explores past interactions for the imprint they have left on man's biological form and current interactions as they influence each individual's growth. Cultural anthropology compares the various institutional and technological responses man has made to the various environments harboring his groups. The relationships between anthropological studies and environmental education are potent and numerous. Only a very few are sketched here.

In archaeology, it is only the fact that man is subject to natural processes that allows his remains to be found. If, indeed, we were independent of the environment and not subject to its cycles, not literally made of it, we might simply cease to exist upon death, or on the other hand never cease to exist at all, remaining thoroughly intact and eternal. In either of these cases archaeology would be out of business. A real dig shows that we are as much at the mercy of time as any other parts of the environment. An imaginary dig can only be engaged in by considering just how our own remains and those of our goods will react to environmental processes. Archaeology is great medicine for anyone believing that our garbage simply goes away.

Physical anthropology can be the science of one-half the man-environment interface, exploring the environment's physical effects on man. From an evolutionary perspective it can be the science of natural selection on human populations: the molding of man's body and the shaping of his races by past environments. In the perspective of the present, physical anthropology shows the shaping of man by his current environments. Effects of nutritional extremes are demonstrable within the confines of this country and within the confines of any urban region. If visits to observe the extremes are too real, at least public records and officials can be consulted to see that the molding hand of environment still rests on man.

Cultural anthropology holds a crucial position in environmental education. Whether presented at elementary or secondary levels, and preferably presented throughout the grades, cultural anthropology opens the study of a most important store of information. It always has been, but is now more than ever important that non-Western cultures, values, and institutions be given great attention and respect. They must be evaluated as alternate responses to environment and must be judged on the success of their maintenance of humanity and environmental balance. Too often other cultures are treated as curiosities having no particular relevance to our own lives. An active search for sound environmental attitudes and values among these cultures is very much in order. Class experiments in employing such attitudes may be first steps toward the formulation of a positive environmental ethic for the school and community.

Biology

The study of bacterial growth in a closed dish or the viewing of a movie of cancer research can provide the most effective images of "unlimited" growth in a limited space. The genetics of fruit-fly populations show that the environment and living organisms are one. The biochemistry of human respiration shows man to be as cyclic inside as the environment is outside. The biophysics of respiration illuminate the fleeting hold we and other organisms have on the sun's energy ration. It is fortunate that the one science that the majority of students study is the source of so many striking encounters with environmental principles. It is unfortunate that biology is so often reduced to a game of words in the scientific tongue.

Biology may be studied according to any number of conceptual schemes, and it is difficult to understand how any one such scheme can be intrinsically better suited to organize biological thought. In a five-week summer course I led a high-school class in an inquiry that has independently been used as a framework for a half-year section of a biology class in a Massachusetts high school. Under the pressure of a five-week schedule, the inquiry succeeds in summarizing human ecology. Over a half year, it becomes an ecological approach to biology. I believe it could as easily be studied over a full year and provide entrance to most major areas of biological interest, which could be independently explored by students and teachers depending on individual preference and resources. Though it is hoped that the course will aid students in sharpening their ecological sense, the goals that I proposed for it in the summer were to find the answers to these questions: Does man's present population constitute a biological problem? And does man's population growth also constitute a biological problem?

The inquiry proceeds roughly as follows:

> How is Earth different from the moon, Venus, Mars, and the rest, and what role does life play in Earth's character? (A question to be raised throughout the course.)
>
> What is a species population? (Requiring investigation into taxonomy, evolution, genetics, and the ecological concept of "niche.")

> How does environment affect organisms? (Requiring investigation into evolution and basic physiology, with access then afforded to biochemistry.)
>
> How do organisms affect environment? (Emphasizing the effect of behavioral adaptations and community succession, providing partial answers to initial questions about Earth.)

The above questions constitute the first half of the course and should involve experimentation and contact with nonhuman species. In effect, this is a basic consideration of principles of environmental biology.

The second half proceeds to concentrate on man:

> Is man a species living in species populations? (Basic human genetics, racial variation, and demography.)
>
> What has been the effect of environment on man? (Basic human evolution and current adaptability of man to environmental conditions.)
>
> What constitutes the human niche? (Basic human physiology, cultural evolution, extension of niche area through microclimates and extension of niche demands through civilization.)
>
> What has been the effect of man on environment? (Study areas are a dime a dozen.)
>
> What are the dynamics of the human population? (Human population history seen in comparison to the organisms studied in the first half of the course.)
>
> What, again, are the effects of environments on man? (A final return to the feedback man is receiving from his own alteration of environment. Are human values suited to an all-human world?)

The entire second half of the course is intended to reflect back to the first half. Insofar as man may be a species (depending upon how the class answers the initial question of the second half), how does he participate in the same environment with other species?

Whatever scheme a biology course follows, the study of life harbors responsibilities in environmental education similar to those held by cultural anthropology. In the way living specimens or dead dissection specimens are treated in biology, lessons are taught about the relative values and respect due the variety of living organisms. If frogs for dissection, no matter how humanely pithed or preserved, are spoken of simply as teaching aids and never once observed or considered in their own right as tenants of Earth, then students will at the very least be misinformed. At the other extreme, if live animals are never brought into the classroom and, equally, if the class never studies a nonhuman living community outside the school, environmental awareness, concern, and competence will be just that much further from a student's grasp.

A problem by no means common only to biology, but of great importance as it occurs in that study, is the use of the concept "natural resource." The initial implications of the phrase are positive: we think of our wisdom in recognizing something as a resource, of the concern we give to wise management of such a resource. But the connotation that any natural resource is a resource for man, for his use only and subject only to his management, contributes to our environmental misunderstanding. To counter the religious support that the resources-for-man notion receives, I would quote the equally religious notion of the great teacher Louis Agassiz, as he wrote in 1873: "The study of nature is an intercourse with the highest mind. You should never trifle with nature. At the lowest her works are the works of the highest powers—the highest something, in whatever way we may look at it." To speak of living organisms as natural resources, is to risk, whether intentionally or not, communicating the environmental myth that the service of man is the highest purpose of Earth. That myth, the sloth king's idea of dominance, inverts all that is known of the environment, which teaches that the service of Earth is the highest purpose of man.

Chemistry

In the wilds of late elementary school I was seduced into liking chemistry by a marvelous book, *Our Friend the Atom,* by Heinz Haber. I still recall the images of chemical realities made exciting by the text and illustrations: a pea in the center of a major-league baseball park representing a nucleus, while the nearest electron shell had to be just outside the center-field fence; all the molecular and atomic space removed from all the battleships in the world's navies, leaving them a solid mass the size of a softball but maintaining all their tonnage. Equally vivid and more inspiring was the image chosen to represent the flow of atoms throughout the Earth. We readers were asked to contemplate that within our bodies, during our lifetimes, would reside atoms that had once been parts of Caesar, Shakespeare, Napoleon; in short, we carried elements of the greatest men the world has known. The study of chemistry is particularly suited to enlarging on this last lesson.

While we are carrying elements from such great personages it is equally probable that we carry a share of the composition of animals now extinct, forests now cut, bombs now exploded. And depending on their persistence, we carry shares of synthetic compounds newly created by man: pesticides, herbicides, gasoline additives, food preservatives, antibiotics. The lesson of chemistry is that the environment is chemical reactions, that we are chemical reactions, and that whenever new compounds or concentrations of elements are released into the environment, they are released in us. As with archaeology, chemistry can dramatically demonstrate that organism and environment are one.

The methods of chemical analysis provide excellent means of seeing environmental relationships. In fact, whole sections of chemistry courses can be oriented around the initial detection and identification of locally problematic pollutants. To take an example that is endemic to our nation, let alone particular localities, a chemistry class can center on the properties of detergents. From analysis of the action and composition of typical detergents, schemes for qualitative and quantitative identification can be planned. These analyses can then be applied to commonly used commercial detergents from students' homes. The action of home washing and transmission through the local sewage disposal or treatment system can be simulated in the laboratory, observing the ultimate state of the compounds as they reenter the hydrologic cycle. Basic, important principles of chemistry cannot help but be discussed and applied in such endeavors. The aid of health and biology classes can be enlisted to discover if the compounds are damaging and in what ways.

Besides the opportunities to follow such a problem-oriented approach, chemistry also affords some of the most striking models of the condition of the biosphere. The study of equilibrium, of the maintenance of an overall system through microscopic actions and interchanges among its components, parallels the study of Earth's living system. A sealed flask in the chemistry lab can also exhibit the limitations that sphericity imposes on this planet. To quote from Frank Herbert's *Dune*, the story of the struggle to reshape the ecology of a desert planet:

> Beyond a critical point within a finite space, freedom diminishes as numbers increase. This is as true of humans in the finite space of a planetary ecosystem as it is of gas molecules in a sealed flask. The human question is not how many can possibly survive within the system, but what kind of existence is possible for those who do survive.

Chemistry can also be a setting for the development of skills necessary to follow causal webs. In fact, to study man's use of petrochemicals without employing such skills is likely to reinforce our traditional, inadequate cause-effect thinking. I recall the plastics industry being discussed in the optimism of the early sixties as the near complete triumph of man over nature: the production of indefinitely durable compounds. In the same chemistry class, we learned that the world depended for its very life-supporting existence on the flexibility and interchangeability of chemical compounds. Somehow we never connected plastics to this life-supporting chemical system. Now that plastics are being detected in the fatty tissues of Arctic birds, having no apparent metabolic role other than the potential stimulation of cancer growth, our lack of foresight seems remarkable, if not tragic.

Earth Science

The effort of Earth science curriculum developers to move beyond classical geology into the field of Earth systems study has set a striking example and should be a rallying movement for all other disciplines. Particularly commendable is the current inner-city program development of the Earth Science Curriculum Project, whose focus on immediate environmental conditions and processes is certainly not applicable only to the inner city.

One section of the inner-city course concentrates on evidence of change. Students collect and monitor, often with the aid of cameras, observable signs of change in the materials and structure of their own neighborhood. The materials are brought into labs for analysis. The geologic and chemical processes contributing to such change are developed on the bases of the collected evidence. With an open-ended approach, these activities can be the best of environmental educations. The participation of man's constructed environment in the processes of the outer environment is evidence of the man-environment interface and provides ready access to it even in a brick picked up from an empty lot. The interface can then be examined for man's passive role, submitting to environmental processes, and his active role, effecting change in the environment, and for the feedback connections that force man's reshaping by his own activities.

Such an investigation lends itself, simply, to the environment, whether it be urban, suburban, agricultural, or "wild." Something that is typically unobserved by students can occupy their most serious study and lead to the connection of their own lives to environmental processes. To quote from one of the ESCP bulletins: "The Environmental Studies [inner-city] Program is not a program *about* an environment. It is a program *in* an environment." And its basic approach can be used in the environment of any locality.

Earth science with a geologic emphasis provides a good framework for raising the question of man's identity. Since man has for so long been the dominant animate geologic force, it is possible and instructive to treat the condition of the earth as a record of man's behavior. Looking at local changes wrought by man, it is worthwhile to ask whether a natural or geologic force leaving similar effects would be considered a disastrous or a beneficial force. Are there basic principles that can be inferred from the record of man's "Earth works"? Can man tolerate the continued application of those principles, or will he be forced to find some means of redirecting or avoiding them?

As an investigation into the rate at which man has assumed his dominance within the world, it might be of interest to pursue the records of continental drift alongside those of human migration and communication. The rates of drift and of the opening and closing of the intercontinental connections are measured in tens of millions of years. It might be possible to determine the rate of separation using paleontological information. Then, using prehistorical and historical records, compare the subsequent narrowing of the separation by man's systems of transportation. How many local animals and plants have been transported between continents by man within the time of a human generation?

Ecology

The opportunities that a course in ecology offers are as varied as those open to Earth science. The caution that must be raised again about ecology and environmental science is that either may easily be oversold. Such courses run the risk of assuming proprietary rights over the study of the environment, to the exclusion of other courses. If approached on a purely academic basis, ecology also runs the risk of repeating the early performance of its counterpart in higher education, that of ignoring a deteriorating biosphere by concentrating on laboratory exercises.

There is at least one hard-and-fast rule that must apply to an ecology course: it must concern itself in large part with the components and conditions of local ecosystems. Whenever and however possible, an ecology course should be centered around the study of a local ecosystem. Academic coverage should not be allowed to prevent in-depth field study and involvement in environmental health action in the school's surrounding area. The communication lines between such a course and other courses in the school should be strong and well used. Students in an ecology course should be able to provide information useful in other studies, in school, district, and neighborhood planning.

An interesting experiment for an ecology class would be to embark on a full-scale environmental inventory, evaluation, and adjustment for the class such as that sketched for classrooms in general in part two, chapter one. Such a class can propose classroom, school, district, and community guidelines toward rational environmental policies. Ecological principles can certainly be learned, and can later on be more easily applied, through the study of the classroom niche and its extensions.

Purely academic bookwork ecology is not likely to catch on. With high-school students it will almost certainly self-destruct from the fact that simply reading and writing about ecology can be one of the dullest exercises imaginable. The relationships are difficult to verbalize. Important concepts are truly complex conceptual schemes, such as "species population" or "niche." Though a course based solely around paperwork on ecology is not likely to last long, there is the danger that it will inhibit a student's further efforts to investigate environmental relationships. Taking on the teaching of "the environment," so titled, is taking on a grave responsibility. Somehow the environment must be met, listened to, and worked with, rather than relegated to ditto sheets and textbooks.

Economics

It was no coincidence that led to the use of the Greek root *oikos* in both "economics" and "ecology." It has been tragic, however, that man ever saw a need for two separate terms. The economies of nature and man are inseparable. Our expansion to 3½ billion, and particularly the Western world's industrialization, have succeeded temporarily by following some rules of nature's economy to the neglect of others. We are just now beginning to feel the effects of these neglected rules of nature's economics.

Sooner or later the economic goals of the Western world will have to be adjusted away from unlimited growth in order to survive exposure to the ills of such growth. What effect this reorganization of the Western economy will have on the goals of the developing world may well depend on how soon the West is able to change. The overextension of population is greatest in the developing world; the longer we wait, the harder the developing world will fall. Deciding for a goal of stability now, we may have a fair chance of easing all mankind's transition and avoiding a suicidal collapse of any large segment of our overlarge population.

Whether economists are able to lead the change of goals or not, it is important that they try not to prevent such a change. At the very least, the teaching of growth economics in schools must be accompanied by some flexibility. There are economists such as Ezra Mishan who have recognized the strangling growth of "disamenities" and "diseconomies" that accompanies unlimited economic growth. Mishan's side should at least have a hearing. A more constructive approach is to attempt to locate, for a given item or service, the costs to the environment (as if they were not costs to man) that are not calculated in its market value. Taking on this task, economics can become as much of a field course as a theory course, because the uncounted costs will have to be evaluated by the class itself.

A yet more constructive approach involves cooperation with an ecology or Earth science class to move from the calculation of environmental costs to consideration of which elements of economic theory are in need of restructuring. Perhaps schoolwide tests of such restructuring would be possible. Ultimately a proposal could be made to the school district and community, at least calling their attention to the current conflicts between economic practice and ecological reality.

Ethnic Studies

Here and there statements are made that the environmental issue is a cop-out, a blind to keep hysterical white America from either seeing or meeting its important responsibilities. Certainly the environmental issue can be such a cop-out, but certainly environmental realities operate irrespective of species, let alone races. The environment has everything to do with America's social responsibilities.

Overuse and overgrowth, in their various institutionalized forms, have been the prime forces behind racial exploitation. The manipulation of a people, whether as slaves or as an economic class, allows another cost to go uncounted, allows a finished product to sell for slightly less than otherwise, and pushes the environmental balance slightly farther off center. The wholesale moving of a people has forced thousand-year adaptations to the land to stumble into completely new environments. Thus, the Great Plains were stripped of a great ecosystem; thus the sickle-cell anemia defense of tropical Africans against malaria was rendered a problematic genetic disease.

The problems with traditional economics mentioned in the preceding section have obvious significance for groups badly in need of economic assistance and development. An ethnic studies program should give consideration to the problems that overgrowth is encountering. An economic future based on expected unlimited overall growth is less likely to be realized with every increase in population and decrease in resources.

Finally, the old ways of land use and the old styles of life, studied in light of ecology, have significant if not ultimately saving contributions to make to the reordering that is at hand. Where the balance will be struck in the end cannot yet be determined, but the industrialized nations are presently far too removed from the land that feeds them, far too addicted to exploitation. The mere existence of ethnic groups speaks of the stability the world once had through diversity of land use. With every additional spread of Western industrial monoculture, this stability is undermined.

General Science

General science is included here mainly to voice a caution against old environmental mannerisms. The general science course itself can make use of ideas presented for any of the other sciences. The caution has to do with the way in which the concept "science" is treated.

Science is often presented to students and the general public as man's battleground with the forces of nature. Scientists, hard at work cracking nature's secret codes, are spoken of as allowing us ever greater mastery over nature, ever more safe and convenient lives. If science had not taught us better about itself, these concepts would be as good as any. But we do know science better, and we can see the implications of our traditional concept and application of science.

Perhaps it is always best to start a general science class with observation of simple living organisms. They have two principal information systems by which they use and react to their environment: a genetic system and a nervous system. The former places limits on their overall sensitivity and may also provide them with stereotyped behavior patterns suited to particular stimuli. The latter, with greater or lesser sophistication, allows faster reaction to a changing environment and perhaps learning through a series of such reactions. Science is this latter activity.

Man's nervous capacity is such that he can consciously explore his environment to a degree unprecedented in the animal kingdom. Combined with communication and cooperation among his fellows he has been able to extend his perception and understanding far beyond limits otherwise programmed into his genetic information system. He has been able to use environmental principles and materials in ever more intricate ways. But conscious exploration and use of the environment do not imply mastery over the environment or freedom from it.

While science has been demonstrating ever more intricate ways of using the environment, it has also been demonstrating how intricately we are connected to the environment. As we have extended our use of the environment, we have inevitably extended our connections to it. We are certainly no freer from the environment now than at any time in our past. We may, in fact, be less able to adapt to unexpected change.

Perhaps general science students can do science, can explore the connections between themselves and the environment, without having to learn the unscientific myth that science provides mastery over nature.

Geography

Boundaries are becoming increasingly troublesome in this overpressured world. Space and resources are every country's problems, while political boundaries have been assumed to limit each country's options for solutions. Environment, of course, recognizes no such boundaries, making boundary-based solutions into problems in themselves.

Some program for reorganizing societies around the form of the environment is essential to the survival of a billionfold human population. To indicate the need for such a reordering and to explore ways of working it out should be the goals of geographical education. Political boundaries will be of increasing importance in human affairs so far as they conflict with environmental system boundaries. A geography class can throw both political and environmental boundaries into sharp relief by examining the disparities between the two.

To study the countries of Africa, then separately to study the river basins of Africa without looking hard at the inherent conflicts is to perpetuate a misunderstanding of the environment. Whose is the Nile? Ethiopia, the Sudan, Egypt, and others lay claim to it. As each country grows it demands more from the Nile. As the upper reaches of the Nile's watershed are exploited, less and less Nile is available to those downstream. Perhaps the Nile rightfully belongs to the countries of the eastern Mediterranean, whose fish catch is dependent upon Nile-supplied nutrients, which nutrients have recently been seriously interrupted by Egypt's Aswan Dam. Perhaps, even more rightfully, the peoples of the Middle East and northern Africa belong to the Nile. In that case, the boundaries of the Nile's tributary system should define a political entity, whose object would be careful treatment of the Nile, bringing its population and economy within the bounds of the river's capacity.

River systems are environmental phenomena that do tend to define boundaries on the land. The overall hydrologic cycle that governs rivers, however, respects no such boundaries, whether political or riverine. Similarly the winds upon which all people depend mix the atmosphere over borders, mountain ranges, even oceans. The air pollution generated in the Los Angeles basin is known occasionally to spill over all southern California, into Nevada and Arizona, even into Utah.

Perhaps a geography class can devise a map similar to that showing the supposed connection of Eastern and Western Hemisphere continents before continental drift. Such a map shows the fit of the present continental shelves, highlighting overlaps and gaps between the shelf lines. On the basis of water alone a map could be devised showing the environmental fit between water-system boundaries and political boundaries. Where do many countries rely on the same water system? Where does a complete system fall within the bounds of a single country? A good follow-up question would be: Where are current trouble spots between nations in relation to the areas of environmental overlap? Finally, how do governmental boundaries fit with environmental systems in the school's own region?

History

When written records were not kept by a culture, we are forced to trace their history in large measure from the marks they left on the environment. Archaeologists deduce technologies, social systems, even rates of development from the alterations left in the land and its life. Admittedly, such inferences are not always accurate and usually not subject to rigid testing. But important aspects of cultures are disclosed in the environmental effects that have, in many cases, outlasted the cultures themselves.

Where written records are available we have tended to leave behind or at least to deemphasize the importance of the unwritten records left in the environment. The drama, poetry, and philosophy of the Greeks are allowed to overshadow their environmental practices. We learn of the treaties and politics that stole the American continent from its native inhabitants, but we give only a passing reference to the swift deterioration of the continent's lands that ensued. The written records are valuable, to say the least, but the conditions of the environment resulting from a civilization's practices have as much to tell us.

Could there not be a history of the American continent, from pre-Columbian times to the present, focusing on the environmental changes that occurred in particular places? The ideal place to begin would be the school's own location. A school in a more recently "civilized" area can spend most of its time in studying the history of other regions, but to start with the immediate locality is still important. At each major alteration in the environment, the question can be raised: What local or national policy or international state of affairs led to this change? Proceeding from environmental effect to the policy that led to the effect would be most illuminating. It would be discovered, for instance, that a city was built on prime agricultural land in order to be close to prime agricultural land. Does the land still exist, or has it been swallowed by the city's own growth? Do lands more recently settled in the West reflect any changes in environmental policies compared to the early eastern settlements? In studying world history, a river provides a good focal point. What has been the history of the Jordan, the Mekong, the Rhine, the Congo? Such a history need not follow any one culture completely coherently. It can follow the important cross-cultural interactions that have shaped and continue to shape the human world.

History classes have an important opportunity to educate about population. The current daily increase in human numbers, about 180,000, challenges the importance of any other historical event, even though it goes unnoticed and certainly unheadlined. Whether for the specific country or region under study, or for the world, each history class should keep some sort of record of the increase in mankind. Consider one week's total increase for the world, 1,260,000: roughly the equivalent of the city of Detroit or of Philadelphia, only with an average age of 3½ days. One would think such an event deserves a weekly headline at least.

Good enough statistics are available for our own United States population to allow the planning of a wall-chart population history of the United States. Use a large enough map so that major urban areas are fairly easily located. The most useful census data starts with 1790, but even earlier records can be used. From 1790 to 1970 gives a 180-year spread. This approximates the number of school days in a full school year, so that weekly intervals correspond roughly to five-year periods. The first move, perhaps a good first-day activity in fact, would be to somehow get 3,900,000 people indicated, by pins, tacks, stars, or other means, in the land area of the original thirteen states, with 5 percent in cities. Though census figures are not available for five-year intervals, an easy estimate can be made, which for 1795 would indicate an increase of about 700,000. The third week would start with another increase of 700,000 and a shift to 6 percent in cities.

This activity can be expected to be a sleeper. Students are likely to be bored with its early stages. If it can be kept up to the end of the year, however, interest is almost guaranteed to pick up. No matter what unit is originally chosen, whether 100,000 per thumbtack or 500,000 per pin, noticeable and problematic changes are bound to take place at an accelerating rate. Taking 500,000 per pin, for instance, the increase from 1940 to 1945 will require the addition of 19 pins to a map already covered by 261, 56 percent in urban concentrations. In the remaining five weeks, 120 pins will have to be added, reaching a temporary 1970 total of some 400 pins, about 70 percent in urban areas. Your map will be a much-confused picture of its former self, but it will have shown the dynamics of our population growth. Perhaps some figures can be found for a companion project, tracing the numbers and locations of the American Indians throughout the same period.

Physics

One of the most important principles controlling the world's ecology has been known to physicists for generations. Lately, ecologists have been given to stating it as "There is no such thing as a free lunch." It combines the notions that all processes involve energy transfer and that energy transfer is never 100 percent efficient. The study of energy in physics can provide an important environmental education.

It is commonly thought that mankind's agricultural revolution has greatly increased the efficiency of energy use. By massive artificial irrigation and fertilization, and by massive distribution to centers of population, it is assumed that man is beating life at its own game, the capture and transfer of energy. In the discussion of the principles of energy and of semiclosed systems, in physics, the validity of these assumptions can be explored.

Where has most of the energy come from to power industrialized agriculture? What is the efficiency of man's fertilization, plowing, irrigation, harvesting, and transport programs per unit of available food energy, compared to the efficiency of nonindustrialized agriculture? What are the effects of the waste energy that escapes in the above programs on the energy budget of the planet and on the planet's temperature?

Physics also has the capability, like chemistry, of equipping students with sensing devices and experimental methods that can be used to test the school's and community's environmental conditions. With every atmospheric nuclear test, no matter by what nation, a Geiger counter becomes a more important tool in environmental education.

Physics cannot be taught or learned without extensive use of models. An ability to improvise and experiment with models is essential to any planning of environmental action. The effort to construct an Earth model, in fact, can be of benefit to the whole school's efforts, and the basic principles of physics are certainly the proper starting points for modeling both the animate and inanimate world.

Psychology

The study of behavior is the study of environmental interaction. Psychologists have long realized that environmental conditions influence personal behavior and that personalities are parts of each other's environments. A game that has been played for centuries, and whose solution is never more than a riddle, is the attempt to discover the boundary between individual and environment. The number and subtlety of the causal links always conspire to break any such imagined barrier. To experiment to find the separation between individual and environment is an instructive and frustrating endeavor.

If we know anything about the environment that fostered the evolution of man, we know that it was highly complex and swiftly changing. It made cooperation, communication, and forethought into great advantages. Much recent popular writing on the nature of man has affirmed that his psychological ills and social incapacities are due to his construction of an artificial environment in which his original attributes are no longer required. It would be interesting to explore in a psychology class whether or not this might be a half-truth of the same type that holds that man has gained supremacy over nature. May it not be the original behavioral attributes that are sorely needed to avert ecological disaster? As we meet nature in more subtle forms, such as our own sewage returned in our drinking water, may we not find that we have never really left that environment that demands cooperation, communication, and forethought?

Psychology classes can also take up the question of optimum population. Experts are meeting these days to determine the biological or physical carrying capacity of the planet. What is the psychological optimum for human population? Do students find they need ever more opportunity to meet human beings or are there already plenty with which to establish relationships? Do psychology experiments on crowding indicate that the current distribution of 3½ billion people exceeds the optimum in many localities?

In the local community, what have been the psychological effects of growth? Has a booming population been a mentally healthy one? What might be the psychological effects of various forms of economic or population controls? Do the psychological effects of overgrowth itself lead to behavioral changes that may make official controls of overgrowth unnecessary?

Sociology

Sociology, studying man's institutions, can throw light on the problem of responsibility for environmental deterioration. Institutions extend each individual's reach into the environment at the same time that they insulate each individual from it. How is it that institutions seem only responsible to secure goods and services for individuals? Was there ever a capacity for conscience, forethought, or self-regulation built into social institutions to keep track of effects on the environment not directly related to the institution's planned functions? How can such an institution be devised? Does a school have the capability of becoming such an environmentally responsible institution?

How have changes in environmental conditions affected the operation of social institutions? It would be interesting to study the effects of population growth on bureaucratic efficiency. Perhaps an institutional optimum population can be determined as manpower and variety gradually conflict with inefficiency. The school district and local government can provide excellent case studies.

Sociology can devote special attention to population studies. Again, the local community and its development policies may provide the best case study. What are the influences of local social institutions on population attitudes and population growth? Good questions for a house-to-house survey are: Do you believe world population growth is a problem? Do you believe family planning is a valuable service? Do you believe population controls should be instituted in the nation or the local community? Do you believe foreign aid should be made conditional upon the foreign country's institution of population limitation?

Charting of population growth can be an asset to any sociology class. One possibility is to follow the changes in world population density since 1650. A wall chart representing a square mile, perhaps mapped for some locally recognizable area, can be set up for a period of thirty-two weeks. Each week then represents a decade, each school day two years, in the 320-year period from 1650 to 1970. Some sort of standardized representation of a human being can be used, and the chart can be filled up something like this:

> 1st week: start with 10 (1650: 500 million/50 million sq. mi.).
> 2nd week: add 1.
> continue to add 1 every other week through week 20 (1850: 20/sq. mi.).
> week 21: add 2.
> continue to add 2 each week through week 25 (1900: 30/sq. mi.).
> week 26: add 3.
> week 27: add 3.
> week 28: add 4 (1930: 40/sq. mi.).
> week 29: add 5.
> week 30: add 5 (1950: 50/sq. mi.).
> week 31: add 10 (1960: 60/sq. mi.).
> week 32: add 14 (1970: 3,700 million/50 million sq. mi.; 74/sq. mi.).

These figures are computed excluding the land area of Antarctica, but making no significant allowance for the other uninhabitable lands on the Earth. The average world population density for 1970 is closely matched by the states of Wisconsin, Louisiana, New Hampshire, and Georgia. It is approximately twice the densities of Arkansas and Texas.

Chapter Two

The Interpreters

It is likely that communication, aesthetic judgment, and creative expression all trace back to the accomplishment of a common purpose with environmental awareness: success in shaping and using the environment for food and shelter. Perhaps there was a time when all art was expected to exert some power to benefit man, such as the luring of game animals, the bringing of rain, or the strengthening of morale to meet an enemy. Aesthetic judgment may have been a matter of evaluating the relative success of the art in achieving its purpose. Communication may have been restricted to the sharing of information on location of game, methods of hunting, and other important environmental phenomena.

The skills of abstraction, imagination, and communication are no longer so clearly directed toward a common goal. Man's capacity for environmental awareness, which was originally enhanced by abstraction and communication, has been dulled by the products of abstraction and communication. As Loren Eiseley has written, ". . . in the attempt to understand his universe, man has to give away a part of himself that can never be regained—the certainty of the animal that what it senses is actually there in the shape the eye beholds."

The development of creative and communicative powers in man's mind parallels the development of man's dominance in the environment. As the sheer size and activity of the human population have made man the single most important biological influence among the world's species, so the sheer complexity of the human conscience has made man's thought the single most important influence on his own behavior. The world is, for better or worse, in our hands, and we are, equally, in the power of our own minds. Again, in the words of Loren Eiseley:

> The terror that confronts our age is our own conception of ourselves. Above all else this is the potion which the modern Dr. Jekylls have concocted. As Shakespeare foresaw:
>
> > It hath been taught us from the primal state
> > That he which is was wished until he were.
>
> This is not the voice of the witches. It is the clear voice of a great poet almost four centuries gone, who saw at the dawn of the scientific age what was to be the darkest problem of man: his conception of himself.

The arts have come to describe the environment man sees within himself as well as the one he sees outside. Our conventions and habits of communication have come to make certain environmental relationships difficult to express and hence easy to overlook. Aesthetic judgments applied to creative works seem no longer to bear relevance to the nonhuman environment. All these developments in man's intellect have come to dominate his conceptions of himself and his environment.

The study of the interpreters offers both a great challenge and a great opportunity. The challenge is to locate the conventions, modes, habits, and rules that block or misdirect environmental awareness and that conflict with the understanding of the environment being worked out by the observers. The opportunity is to build new forms and expressions that can sharpen environmental awareness and can communicate a new understanding of environment and man.

Art

The history of art is a history of man's relations with the environment. From primitive through both Western and non-Western civilizations art shows the role of environment in the lives of men and betrays their prevailing assumptions about environmental laws. It would be interesting to include in a survey of the art of our time not only the important modern styles of painting that hang in galleries and museums but the department-store landscapes that hang in so many private homes. Such mass-produced paintings of rural scenes or glittering coastal sunsets display intriguing combinations of environmental realism and environmental nonsense in their proportions and colors.

An important question for an art class to consider, if not to answer, is: What is aesthetically pleasing or displeasing about an environment? Why are certain natural environments considered more beautiful than others? Why are so many human creations considered ugly? We tend to make judgments and accept them easily about neighborhoods, buildings, parks, beaches, calling them beautiful or ugly. But what is it about these environments that is being subjected to our aesthetic judgment? Is it naturalness? Is it functionality, itself a form of naturalness? Or is it some collection of proportions and distributions that are given a priori aesthetic status? Our earliest aesthetic conceptions probably had a great deal to do with protection and productivity in a demanding environment, but on what are they based now?

Artists crusade for freedom of individual expression and champion individual diversity. This diversity is in great part dependent on diversity of experience, which is based upon availability of diverse environments. What is the meaning, for an artist, of the extinction of a species, or the substitution of an apartment complex for a forest? Is there a limit to the diversity possible among artists if the Earth's environmental diversity is seriously reduced?

To express himself the artist must use the environment, whether in the form of a canvas, paper, clay, ink, paints, or the heat to fire clay. For early man, obtaining a bone, mixing dyes, or building a fire was a difficult and demanding task. A great respect for the environment, if not a reverence for it, still exists among people who put such effort into the securing of their materials. For the Bushman of the Kalahari, the time and the effort to produce rock paintings have simply become unavailable as these people have been forced into the more severe reaches of their desert environment. Buying paper and paints in a store is not the same sort of experience. The connection between modern-day artist and environment can be distant indeed. Whenever possible, art students should make their own materials, that is secure them from the environment, before they use those materials as vehicles for their own expression. In cases where this borders on the impossible, as with production of paper, a field trip to the source is in order. A visit to a forest and a discussion of how it is possible to derive paper from trees begins to place a value on sketch pads or posterboard that no classroom lecture or art-store price tag can adequately convey.

Finally, are there particular art forms that can communicate environmental realities especially well? Photography, for example, has assumed the burden of showing us the scars of man-created environments. The photographic medium, however, can distance the observer even further from the environment. Seeing the photograph is often taken as equivalent to having been there, so the visit may never be made. What would be the effect of an Andrew Wyeth of our dead rivers, smoking cities, and strip mines? Would the patience required to produce such paintings allow them to communicate environmental realities more deeply than coolly objective photographs?

Creative Writing

Creative writing bears many of the same relationships to the environment as are explained above for art. Variety of environmental experience is at least as crucial to the freedom of the creative writer. The writer's materials have been extracted from the environment in the same way as any artist's and deserve similar respect. Pencils are often mistaken for being expendable; seldom are they seen as thin cylinders of the hundred-million-year-old bodies of organisms not known to man, wrapped in the tissue of a recently killed tree.

Writing takes us far into the inward environment of man's words and habits of speech. Using these human constructs to describe the natural environment takes a writer to the very crux of the problem of environmental misunderstanding. We usually have no adequate means of describing relationships we have been slow to recognize. To speak clearly of the oneness or of the interconnections in nature is very difficult indeed. Usually some agrammatical juxtaposition of words in a poetic form is more successful than a traditional prose exposition.

The writer who forces himself to deal with this problem of expressing the conventionally inexpressible may be more equipped than anyone else to see the important gaps in our environmental understanding. It would be interesting to spend time in a natural habitat and then to attempt a creative exposition of observations and principles. A discussion of those most difficult to write about and an investigation into why they prove so difficult might turn up important conclusions about the relative estrangement of man from his environment.

The effort to describe natural principles can also lead to the formation of new artistic and grammatical conventions suited to a deeper environmental understanding. Creative writing has always been an important source of environmental philosophy and even of secondhand exposure to the real environment. It may well become the most important vehicle for communication of our growing environmental understanding.

Drama

Acting can be a major exercise in environmental awareness. Especially in the form of improvisation without aid of props or set, acting becomes a re-creation of an environment through the expression of the environment's imprint on the individual. One cannot adequately react to an invisible environment unless one has spent considerable time observing environmental effects and analyzing sensory responses. Then, through projection of reactions to imaginary stimuli, an actor makes the environmental sources of the stimuli become "visible" to his audience.

Such improvisational acting is an especially good environmental exercise if it is restricted to worldless mime. Without benefit of any verbal description, then, the actor and the audience are both required to use only their own environmental sensitivities. The mimes, in turn, can be restricted to the use of only one sense at a time: show a forest walk only by displaying visual reactions; show the preparation of a meal only through touch or only through smell. These exercises are highly artificial and highly instructive. To participate in them either as actor or observer necessitates a confrontation with environmental realities that are otherwise almost always taken for granted. Viola Spolin's work, included in the Bibliography (p. 199), is a masterful collection of such improvisational experiments.

Drama also provides two valuable models of environmental realities. The action of putting up a set and costuming a cast, carrying out the play, then resetting and recostuming another play from the same materials can be an excellent example of reuse. It mirrors the succession of living communities, one growing from the decomposed materials of the other. If a dramatic organization is efficient, in fact, it may be the most environmentally sane of all our art forms: it continually reshapes and reuses materials extracted from the environment, creating endless variety from a finite supply.

We may also owe to drama what little comprehension we are able to bring to bear on the interconnecting feedback web of nature. As was mentioned earlier in the discussion of overuse and overgrowth, the Greek tragedians relied on the fact that there are no simple, one-way relationships among people. Their plays have intrigued audiences for centuries because of the subtleties of the causal webs in which their characters live. In a play we speed up and objectify the relationships that are always operating in our own lives, but usually just out of our temporal focus. As players act out these causal webs they show us quite clearly the nature of the environment. The processes of human societies and of ecosystems are one.

English Grammar

The problems discussed above for creative writing have their roots at least in part in English grammar. There are certain environmental relationships for which we lack adequate tenses and cases, let alone adequately descriptive words. We readily form active or passive verbs, for instance, describing actions and reactions. But we realize more and more with further study of the environment that actions are reactions are actions. Something happening is at once active and passive. A grammar class can consider this problem and perhaps try to construct a suitable form for expressing what is now inexpressible.

Our tenses serve to delineate occurrences in the past, present, or future. But, insofar as events are both active and passive and fully interconnected, events are also timeless; they occur in present, past, and future. To say that we built a dam is correct in an extremely limited sense. How can we grammatically indicate that the building of the dam continues to operate in the environment and will continue to exert influence for generations? Might there not be some grammatical inroad made into the reality of the time continuum that supports our actions in past, present, and future?

Another grammatical dilemma is presented by the persons of pronouns. There is truth and considerable convenience in the division of the world into me, you, and it. But there is a truth of equal importance that has no accepted grammatical form: that is, we are all connected through environmental cycles and through the webs radiating from our actions. Therefore, I am you and it; and you both, animate and inanimate, are I. Our present grammatical forms render such expressions just slightly absurd. An ability to convey them with some clarity would go far in helping us deal with the environment. Our actions *are* smog. Smog, as it becomes us, poisons us. The problems of our current grammatical forms and their contributions to environmental misunderstanding can be discussed as they are studied. In absence of better forms or additional ones, awareness of the limitations of current grammar may be the most for which we can hope.

Journalism

The power of the press in bringing the problems of pollution and population to the public has been a mainstay of the current environmental revolution. Earth Day ads have boosted membership in long-standing conservation organizations and have given rise to new ones. Letters columns have proved an important forum for citizen response to environmental problems. Hopefully the papers' role in monitoring the environment will be maintained in coming years. Yet papers are also part of the problem.

An article from the May 31, 1970, *New York Times* raises, in the medium, the medium's own problems: some 10 percent of the solid waste collected daily in New York City is old newspapers; out of the six pounds of paper that comprise a single issue of the Sunday *New York Times,* the average reader reads one-and-a-half pounds; only some 20 percent of the newsprint used once in this country is reused. Newspapers are deeply involved in the problems of waste generation, deforestation, and pulp-mill pollution. And, of course, advertising keeps a paper alive and often amounts to the major share of its bulk. This advertising usually promotes overuse itself.

The immediate action that is available to papers for lessening their adverse environmental impact (and enhancing the impact of their environmental editorials) is the recycling of newsprint. In the recycling of old newsprint, only some 15 percent of the paper is lost, and the resultant product of at least one recycling firm has been found by the *New York Times* to be ". . . of high quality and satisfactory in all respects," while cheaper than fresh newsprint.

School papers, and those of various student and teacher organizations, certainly do not approach the bulk or the circulation of the Sunday *New York Times*. Yet, totaled across the country, their impact is significant. A major environmental service can be performed, then, by school papers. They can contact a recycling plant or bring pressure to bear on a plant that could recycle newsprint. They can initiate a collection of their own and other used issues to sell to the recycling plant. If local garbage collection agencies refuse to contribute the effort of separate pickup, the school can launch its own transportation campaign. Finally, the paper can complete the cycle by rebuying itself from the recycling plant, thereby cutting new paper purchases by 85 percent.

As a model for what school papers can accomplish toward environmental education, there is not likely to be a better example than the April 20, 1970, edition of the University of Washington *Daily,* distributed free to all students and personnel, and sold at a single-copy price of 50 cents. This eighty-page, four-section issue presented the local region, Puget Sound, as an environment through the eyes of faculty, students, public officials, and locally important organizations, commercial and otherwise. The sections were organized as first, an overall summary, "The Environmental Challenge," second, "Pollution and Resources," third, "Urban Growth," and finally, "The University," an important consideration of the role of an educational institution. A secondary school cannot be expected to match the finished style and to reach the readership of this publication, but several lessons can be learned from its format and success. The problems considered are *local*, problems immediately visible and accessible to individual participation. The people drawn upon represent all ages and interest groups, and their inherent conflicts. The summation of the issue considers the role of the institution at hand, the university. This format can be followed by a paper on that paper's own scale, and the relative circulation can match that of the university's effort: originally scheduled for 25,000, at least 50,000 were finally published to accommodate outside orders. Followed by a campaign to regather the papers for recycling, the impact of this kind of journalism on a neighborhood could be significant.

Languages

The study of a foreign language is also the study of a foreign environmental view. The conventions of grammar indicate degrees or kinds of environmental awareness and can be considered in the same way as is proposed for English grammar above. The vocabulary of a foreign language provides an even richer store of evidence for environmental perceptions.

It has become fairly common knowledge that people dependent on wind, for example, have built a rich vocabulary to describe the subtleties of winds. Those of us who have come to act as though we were independent of winds do not have the words to express such subtleties and frequently cannot understand what it is others are seeing. Studying a language, it is interesting to examine vocabulary for richness or shallowness of environmental expression. Our own ability to recognize such richness or shallowness is, of course, dependent upon our own degree of environmental awareness.

In all languages there are common figures of speech that nominally refer to environmental realities, but that are used for widely divergent purposes. Recognizing such figures in our own speech is frequently difficult because we are so accustomed to accept their second-level meanings. In foreign languages they may stand out as, indeed, do most words and phrases with which we are not familiar. A close look at the root meaning of the phrase, its original environmental significance, compared to its commonly accepted meaning affords insight into the evolution of a culture's environmental conscience.

In our own language, an example is the phrase "to the ends of the Earth." Geographically it smacks of the pre-Columbian conception of this planet as some sort of plane with definite, not to mention dangerous edges. We tend to use the phrase to designate some remote region, probably uninhabited by man, and we most often mean to imply we have expended the effort it would take to reach the ends of the Earth. Two things are noteworthy about this usage. First, continued use of the phrase implies that there remain such remote areas as might be called the ends of the Earth. This is interesting because there are far fewer such areas now than when the phrase first came into vogue. It might be better to use the verb "save" rather than "reach" to imply significant effort: "I tried to *save* the ends of the Earth for her." This raises the second problem. The effort to get to one of the remaining remote areas is not the effort it used to be. How many of us have expended anything like the effort of the first explorers by sea and overland journey? And, if we were going to some remote area now, how many of us would choose to deny ourselves the convenience of the internal-combusion engine in all its forms? It is no longer that difficult to get most anywhere. Flying to Little America in Antarctica is little more adventuresome than flying to Minneapolis in midwinter. So the phrase carries two environmental implications that are far out of date.

An interesting transformation of the phrase "to the ends of the Earth" turned up in a recent magazine advertisement. A major oil company involved in the development of the north slope of Alaska no doubt meant to imply to its customers that it was going to great effort, braving the Arctic, to supply their cars with fuel and lubricants. What was actually printed, whether misprint, Freudian slip, or, God help us, intentional was: the company is going ". . . to the end of the earth" to supply its customers with products. On the whole, this new phrase is environmentally more sound and may serve to educate oil consumers about the true price of their consumption. But again, to imply great effort, the company should have said, rather, "to *prevent* the end of the Earth"; for it seems to be far harder for us to refrain from using the oil than to deplete it in a rush.

Literature

Literature continues to be a most important medium for promoting environmental understanding. The web of words, in the hands of a master, can do much to display environmental relationships and qualities. The limitations on words, as discussed under creative writing, English grammar, and languages above, are always of interest as they communicate the environmental assumptions of the age in which they are written.

A course being offered in an elementary school on Mercer Island, Washington, has taken a strongly creative approach both to environmental understanding and the study of literature. Having read an author's description of some setting or animal or some occurrence in nature, the classes set out to locate similar conditions in a semiwild nature-study area adjacent to the school. They are encouraged to bring the author's words to bear on their own experiences and to let each amplify the other. Further, they can then evaluate the success of the author in conveying a picture of a forest, or a river, or the sequence of autumn changes. Did he overlook significant relationships? Did he use both the sound and the meaning of his chosen words to good advantage? Finally, the students are encouraged to build upon the author's and their own perceptions by writing on their own.

Such an approach need not be restricted to schools with nature areas. Experience in natural areas should be available to all students, but the words of the Earth Sciences Environmental Curriculum are worth remembering: the study of literature need not be the study *of* an environment, rather let it be a study *in* an environment. Use the ever-present environment at hand.

It would be interesting to collect passages from literature, or better yet, have students search them out, that describe a particular environmental relationship or phenomenon. Take rain as an easily accessible example. What do writers usually say about rain? Do writers from particular foreign countries have any ways of speaking about it that seem strange or difficult to understand? The class can develop such a series of questions and can consider authors' uses of "rain" to carry certain themes. They can experiment with their own writing. Then, when rain comes, the class can meet it with their own senses of sight, taste, touch, smell, and hearing all turned toward this phenomenon. What are the realities of rain? How far will it ever submit to being described?

Mathematics

It is both oversimplification and understatement to say that population and pollution problems are nothing but rate problems. It is oversimplification because values, histories, economies, religions, and other complexities make up the driving forces behind overuse and overgrowth; understatement because the rates are, indeed, astronomical. If we knew nothing of rates, chances are we never would have achieved our precarious dominance over nature. Only through our understanding of rates have we now got a chance to save nature and ourselves from collapse.

Mathematics is both a powerful language, capable of

informing us about rates, and an art medium capable of portraying our environment as can no other. The environmental revolution has prompted talk of changing all the math problems ever assigned to students to population problems. Ultimately, this might do more to complicate rather than promote the development of awareness, concern, and competence. Advantage should be taken of the powers of mathematics to fill out students' capabilities to deal with the environment, not to overimpress students with environmental problems.

Rather than swamp students with more problems or with problems rewritten to be environmental, time in a math course can be better spent outside the classroom or with classroom projects to explore the realities of rates. Questions similar to those asked in the literature course discussed above might be asked. How well do symbols convey the realities of events? Are there environmental realities that cannot be effectively symbolized? Can students devise better ways for representing phenomena such as densities, growth rates, changes in water composition?

Mathematical formulas are powerful tools for understanding environmental conditions, but they are of even greater use in predicting future environmental states. At the outset of a course one can obtain up-to-date figures on some local population and a record of its growth. Initial study of rates, curves, or graphing then involves plotting the most likely continuation of growth. This can be checked at intervals through the year depending on the size of the population and the availability of the information. Surely a fish tank with a readily available population of animals and plants would be an asset to any math classroom.

Math also provides a good framework within which to consider both the validity and the power of such predictions. Curve projections, and particularly those representing population growth, are too easily accepted as factual representations of the future. They are often presented as descriptions of the way things will be, when they can never be more than descriptions of the way things will be only if certain conditions are met. It should become a rule for all discussions of population growth, whether they be in newspapers, on television, or in schools, that the curve based upon continuance of present conditions should never be presented alone. Always it should be accompanied by curves showing the possible futures of different birth rates or death rates. Presenting only the one curve implies an absolute future, the sort of prophecy that contributes to its own fulfillment.

The symbols and conventions of mathematics also provide a great medium for modeling environmental situations. Some of the most important principles and attendant dilemmas that confront man in the environment can be effectively illustrated in mathematical games. An example was given me recently by a math teacher who saw the "tragedy of the commons," as described by Garrett Hardin, in the game of the Prisoner's Paradox. This game is beautifully displayed in a simple four-square graph of the conditions bearing upon two men accused of a crime. The penalty does not entirely depend upon the individual's plea of guilty or not guilty, but upon the statement made by the other prisoner as well. Ultimately, it is to the relative benefit of both to declare themselves guilty and announce the other's complicity. Their fines are thus moderated, though they also lose the possibility of avoiding fines altogether. As we put greater and greater individual demands on the environment we are making such "middle-road" decisions: my car is of such value to me that I will use it, even though I am forgoing the benefits of a pollutionless world (which would at least be nearer without internal-combustion engines) and am bringing a degree of penalty on myself and all others by operating my car. Middle-road decisions eventually result in conditions that appear, from the outside, absurd, as in the case of the outsider's view of Los Angeles. Still, to an insider, another share of the commons seems to bring him goods enough to outweigh the generalized hardships he causes.

The mutually beneficial situations that often typify natural communities of diverse species can be modeled against the fragile state of a monoculture. Some sort of graphic representation of species' interrelationships can be devised resembling the ecologist's food web. Single-factor alterations can then be made, and the results can be compared for complex systems and for simple systems. Perhaps a class can seek the magnitude of alteration necessary to disrupt a system of a given complexity. A class environmental inventory such as is described in part two, chapter one, ought to provide information for constructing a model of classroom/environment interrelationships which might then be evaluated for their complexity and stability.

Music

Music, like other arts, had environmental beginnings. Especially if man evolved from a stock of tree dwellers before descending to the savanna, it is likely that wide-ranging vocalization was an important asset for staking territories. The most arboreal form of the present ape groups, the gibbon, possesses and uses a range of vocal sounds that is equaled by few of man's instruments.

The meaning of some environmental problems should be of great importance to music students. Probably the most obvious is the growth of noise, with which musicians increasingly have to compete. In a city, outdoor performing areas, even indoor areas, are increasingly plagued by the penetration of traffic and construction noises. Listening to live music may be threatened as much as listening to live birds, and by similar activities.

There is also the simple question of space. It takes room to perform music, especially symphonic music. Some distance to the audience is necessary to experience the whole. But such room is a chunk of environment that may have to be used for freeways, housing units, parking lots. Room to perform music is the kind of luxury that will be the first to go if food and bare survival become man's immediate, rather than simply immanent problems.

As with art and literature, the experiences available to composers are conditions upon their freedom. Bruckner, in the nineteenth century, found his music in the mountains of Germany where today he might find ski resorts and muzak. The late Eric Dolphy built the artistry of his jazz woodwind performances on a lifetime of listening to birds, some species of which may soon go the way of the passenger pigeon. The environment is a variety of songs and sound shapes that has given birth to and nourished man's music. With the passing of wilderness passes the meat of the nourishment.

The revolutions of electrified and then electronic music raise serious environmental questions. A violin, shaped from the substance of a tree, deserves respect and use as any artist's materials do. But the energy to play a violin or guitar is among the cleanest forms, the animal respiration of human cells. An electrified violin, piano, or guitar, however, is cashing in on the hydroelectric dam, the coal generator, perhaps even the nuclear plant. There is a real problem of values here, perhaps more strikingly portrayed by a concert of electric rock music that may be singing of the threatened environment in a city's smog, while the demand for more smog from the coal generator is coming, in part, from the musicians' own instruments.

Plastic instruments raise further problems. Drumheads made from animal skins are increasingly hard to find. Instead, synthetic "skins" are used and deemed better in quality of performance. But what is the use of a better performance if the burning of old drumheads and other plastic instruments has given both audience and performer a load of toxic plastic compounds throughout their bodies?

These are all questions worthy of discussion in music classes. They are also worthy of action. A school band, considering purchase of a new, improved plastic bassoon, might find it reasonable to settle for slightly musically less in order not to clog their Earth with more indisposable plastics.

The action of performing ensemble music itself provides environmental lessons. The whole of a composition is inescapably greater than its parts, while the parts are inescapably essential to creation of that whole. In cooperating to weave a musical performance, musicians are playing an old environmental game. The sound of a trumpet is inescapably colored by the accompaniment of strings. The resulting sound is neither the sound of strings or trumpet. Two "causes" have produced an "effect" that neither could produce alone and that could be produced in no other way. A musical composition, in performance, is a web, a community of sound. The aesthetic judgment to which music is usually subjected can be transferred to the webs of living communities. What is the effect of domination by one instrument? What is the effect of juggling roles without regard to the composer's intent? Can a composition, once performed, ever be performed in quite the same manner? Did Beethoven create for us an international park?

Philosophy

The study of philosophy can be a study of man's history of and capacity for environmental awareness. It can then be a vehicle for enhancing the awareness of the student. Political philosophy from the Greeks to the present is a philosophy of distribution of environmental resources. In the maxims and arguments of political philosophers lie evidences of their awareness of environmental principles. Philosophies of man's nature cannot help but be philosophies of environment's nature as well. The picture painted of mankind by a philosopher, for instance, may indicate more about his understanding of the environment than a treatise specifically given over to "Nature" or some such topic. Epistemologies deal with the environment as they consider man's capacity for knowing the environment. What do these philosophies imply as the important features of the environment? How do they compare with the current teachings of ecology? If various ecological teachings are correct, what would be the environmental effects of pursuing a social order based on a given philosophy?

Perhaps most important for the environment is a consideration of the meaning of responsibility. How far is a man responsible for his actions? If an action conceived for personal gain has to be measured against societal cost, does it also have to be measured against environmental cost? Can social and environmental responsibility really be two things?

Finally, philosophy can be an important forum for trying out a world view. Students can consider the question of life's meaning, which must in some way be based upon a world view. Where do value increments fall along the man-environment continuum? What goals for an individual might be incompatible with the principles of the environment? Are there principles of the environment that, in themselves, seem to obstruct self-fulfillment? Does finiteness restrict freedom?

Reading

The teaching of reading is a great problem. It would be foolish to propose that some revolution in environmental thinking is going to alleviate or eradicate this problem. But from my own experience with reading-problem students of high-school age, I can see one environmental contribution that might help.

At least some of the problems students have with reading are due to overpressure, to the fact that all success in school seems to depend on reading. Students, knowing this through the student grapevine and sensing it in the attention given reading, are put in the position of threatened species in the wild: a slight mishap can eliminate them in their fragile condition. An initial bad start in reading progressively becomes a more serious dilemma. One is cut off from studying with one's peers, which may lead to being cut off from their social nucleus in school. The need for reading help increases, but so does the social stigma of asking for it. And the tension surrounding the whole activity of learning to read becomes inhibitive.

A shifting of emphasis to include *all* our awareness capabilities in schoolwork will be beneficial to these students who have trouble catching up in reading. Further, the deemphasis of reading may lead to a more rational approach to it in the first place. Cannot reading lessons assume a place parallel to lessons in hearing, seeing, touching, and generally sensing the environment? A book can then be presented as an extension of our senses something like a telephone or a telescope. Through it, we are able to sense environments communicated to us by others. A book is not a tool, in fact, that can be used unless we are capable of being aware ourselves and of bringing our own sense experiences to bear on the author's.

Students generally learn to use instruments such as microscopes quite well, with interest, and with growing respect, if not browbeaten with cautions and restrictions. Books, met as instruments, can be used in much the same way. Greatly helping this development of reading as awareness would be a shift away from textbook-assigned reading to textbook-available reading. The writing in many of our most widely used texts is to reading as dry oats are to eating. If material does not contain within itself its own enticement, it should not be assigned; such books should be used as optional information sources. Reading assigned, if ever, should be carefully picked for its style as well as for its content. The beauty of reading and writing as arts lies in the fusion of style and content into an inseparable whole.

Writing

Printing and writing were much maligned in my elementary-school years. We learned to print all right, then we learned to write. But few of us saw these as anything other than time-consuming and irksome tasks. They were presented in much the same manner as reading: as though our lives depended on them. A growth in the use of other forms of communication will hopefully put writing in a clearer perspective as an environmental interaction.

To write is to mark the environment. Writing should be

practiced after students have experienced the burning of wood to produce charcoal, the crushing of leaves to mix inks, or the shearing of rocks to obtain a slate. The tools of writing are extracted from the environment and deserve the same respect and care as those used by the artist. The alphabet and other symbols can then be seen to be made of the environment through the use of writing tools.

The symbols can either grace or deface the environment from which they come. With a bit less haste than usually goes into the learning of writing, the symbols can be treated as works of art in themselves. Students learning to write can evaluate the effect that these symbols, in the name of advertising, have on the environment of their local community. Political action may be initiated by the class to enforce a code limiting use of environmental space for signs.

Chapter Three

The Users

There is no sense in claiming that any classification system completely and adequately shows the relationships between disciplines. It is important, however, to emphasize the "use" function of this last group of subjects. Though all areas of study must use the environment, the connections to environment are more direct for these vocational, recreational, hygiene, and practical courses. Yet many of them are seldom considered as environmental courses in spite of their explicit aim to teach ways of using the environment.

The users have always provided the main practical environmental education in our schools. Curiously and sadly enough they are often looked down upon. They seldom are required for college preparation. When required for graduation from schools they are often only begrudgingly undertaken by the college-bound students. Perhaps this is an informative commentary on our overall environmental attitude: direct, personal involvement with environment, such as is studied and developed in these courses, is not seen as worthy of the same consideration given to the study of intellectual conceptions of the environment. A commitment to environmental rationality must somehow involve a commitment to doing away with this artificial hierarchy of subject prestige.

The users offer important opportunities for making connections between environmental principles, environmental values, and living in present society. Goals for these courses can be basically twofold: (1) to be able to see and to describe everyday conditions and activities as uses made of environment, and (2) to be able to judge the environmental effects of such uses according to our best understanding of environmental principles. In all these courses, major roles should be played by investigation and experimentation, especially since many environmental judgments cannot be made without actively comparing different procedures. There are rich opportunities for fruitful interdisciplinary work with the observers and interpreters.

Agriculture

With every passing second, as more than one unit is added to the human population, it becomes increasingly important for agriculture to be seen as an environmental happening. Agriculture is a very specialized form of participation in the environment. It is founded on environmental principles, yet capable of doing great environmental damage through oversight, ignorance, misinformation, or sheer goodwill for humanity.

The most serious environmental mistake that some teachers, researchers, and practitioners of agriculture make is to spread the gospel of the anticipated green revolution that is to lift man from any threat of famine. Without a doubt the best interests of man and agriculture are in the hearts of those who make these predictions. Yet the optimism generated by such talk, however cheerful, cannot be beneficial. The implication most easily drawn is: If we can feed so many more people, then we can probably feed even more and need never consider limiting our population. The implication is that we are about to receive the biggest free lunch ever conceived. A complex rule of ecology, taken from physics, is expressed simply as "There is no such thing as a free lunch." A corollary is that the bigger the planned lunch, the less free it can possibly be. Perhaps we could afford, in dollars and cents, to accomplish such a green revolution. Environmentally the costs would be unbearable. We would be selling our house for a single meal, while the next livable house is probably light-years away.

A question that at least bears discussion in the learning of agriculture is: Are there already too many people? On a matter-of-fact agricultural basis, the answer is probably No. But the environment did not evolve and does not presently operate on a strictly matter-of-fact agricultural basis, and neither does man. We ourselves have claimed that we do not live by bread alone. It is not likely that we would long resemble a human race if food were all we could look for in the environment, our animal and plant competitors having been largely eliminated. Humanness rests upon our recognition of those animals and plants as companions rather than simply competitors. The step to considering our fellow men as competitors is not a difficult one; in the absence of animal and plant companions the step is all the more easy to take.

Clearly agriculturalists, if they stopped trying to meet present demands for increased production, would be quickly replaced. But agriculturalists can take a major step toward environmental sanity by beginning their own education with the knowledge that human life must depend on population limitation. The goals of agriculture in a limited population are the development of quality of nutrients and the reduction of adverse environmental impact. Certainly agriculture will not stagnate under such declared goals. If research can be centered on these goals now, this clear recognition of environmental needs will go far in educating the general public.

It would be interesting for an agricultural class to calculate for its local area the amount of diversion of the water cycle that would be necessary to meet the food needs of some imaginary future population. What might be the environmental costs of the production, transport, and application of the artificial fertilizers necessary to support such food production? The alternatives of lesser production or of maintaining a steady state should also be calculated. Concurrently, a research project might investigate ways of improving water use, developing reliance on natural fertility, and other activities that might be carried out if the population were to remain stable. What would be the environmental effects of such activities?

The future of farming will in no way be depressed by a stabilization in population. On the contrary, the possibility of moving away from heavily industrialized farming to lessen detrimental environmental impact should greatly increase the demand for agriculture research and for practicing farmers. A stabilizing of demand may allow a move away from monocultures to allow discontinuation of chemical control of insects and weeds. Such a move would also make impossible much mechanical harvesting, further reducing the drain on petroleum and other energy resources. This will require a great influx, however, of farmers willing to undertake the management of such agriculture. If farm prices can be based on quality of food minus environmental damages incurred in the food's production, the market for innovation should make such agriculture highly competitive. If I am not mistaken, urban America is not entirely satisfied with its city life. There are plenty of people who would now return to working the land if they saw, indeed, a future in it. This move toward stabilized demand, lessening of environmental impact, and competition for quality can make the future of farming very secure indeed.

Automotive Shop

There may be no single device that is more crucial to the quality and future of America's environment than the automobile. If any significant changes are to be made to alleviate environmental damage done by man, these changes will have to include alterations in the design, marketing, and regulation of automobiles. If such changes are made within an adequate time, then the basic training of internal-combustion technology will not be sufficient for a mechanic; the changes will occur during his working lifetime.

To prepare for these changes in mode of transportation and perhaps to help stimulate them, automotive shop classes should consider the overall questions of transportation and energy use. Use of energy for transportation provides convenience only at an environmental cost. Some forms of energy use and transportation systems exact greater costs per capita than others. It happens that the costs exacted by the internal-combustion engine powering the private automobile are particularly high, so high in fact that people question whether they do not significantly outweigh the advantages of such transportation.

What are cleaner energy drives for transport vehicles? What are likely to be the mechanical service requirements of such engines? What are more efficient transportation systems in urban areas than the one man–one vehicle system that seems to have given the cities to the vehicles? What aspects of the internal-combustion engines now used are particularly important for the public to know about?

An auto shop can deepen its own investigation into the workings of engines and simultaneously perform a valuable service and educating role for the community by running an emission clinic. The services of the shop students with measuring equipment can be made available to local drivers. Cars can be checked against state or auto shop standards. An effective method of reporting the results might be to hand each driver a qualitative and a quantitative list of the emissions he is releasing into the atmosphere per a mileage or time unit. The members of the shop can perhaps perform tuning adjustments or emission control device repairs.

The shop can, after involvement with pollution measurement and discussion of the transportation problem, take a step similar to that taken by the United Auto Workers Union, which recently challenged its employers' industry with a contract clause demanding the reduction of current engine emissions and the development of nonpolluting engines. Similar requests from future mechanics can help speed the process; if made public, they also can perform a valuable community education function. A statement of concern from those most directly involved with automobile engines can attract a great deal of attention.

Business Education

All of man's business enterprises are means of mediating man's interaction with environment. These enterprises are often described as if their sole intent was to secure individual profit. This represents a narrow oversimplification of a business's goals, which may well include providing for the benefit of man generally. Just as narrow an oversimplification, however, is the common assumption that a business selectively affects the environment, providing one particular convenience or using only one particular resource.

A grocery store may seem only to be providing a central distribution point for food, facilitating the public's nutrition. The storage of such foods brought from varying distances requires use of chemical preservatives that may threaten the public's health. Preservation also requires freezing in some cases, draining electric power from the environment at production, transportation, and storage centers. The transportation of food both to and from the store usually involves a dip into the fossil-fuel supply, along with a contribution to atmospheric contamination. The provision of no-return bottles for public convenience may significantly increase the local waste-disposal problem. The store does not simply sell nutrition to its public; it impinges on the environment in innumerable significant ways.

Some beginning must be made in business education to study business techniques in full consideration of their environmental effects. The terms "side effects" and "by-products" should be eliminated from business curricula. There are no such phenomena in the environment. Those businesses that claim a basis in growth must also deal with their environment's strict limitation: there can be no unlimited growth.

A business education class can undertake to discover

all the environmental connections involved in a given business. It would be useful, also, to question which businesses will be most affected by a serious effort to build rational environmental policies into the American economy. There is every indication that future businessmen and women will be forced into some sort of action by a frightened public if environmental conditions are not improved. In the long run it will make much greater economic and environmental sense for businessmen to explore the ecological significance of their enterprises first and lead the public in restructuring the economy.

In the practice of any secretarial work or in the learning of typing, every effort should be made to recognize environmental interaction and to lessen overuse. The paper used in typing, for instance, deserves as much respect as that used in art or creative writing. The conventions in typing of one-side-only page use and every-other-line spacing deserve as much consideration, and perhaps revision, as school policies covering the writing of papers and themes. For typing practice, used ditto sheets from the schools' other classes can be cycled into reuse.

Models of reuse practices, of new typing conventions, and results of business-in-environment surveys can be brought to the attention of local businessmen and groups. It can be demonstrated, for example, that a short letter can easily be communicated on a short piece of paper, or that a long one is quite readable even if single-spaced on both sides of the page. Free estimates of the amount of overuse that might be eliminated through such practices might be provided to the local businessmen.

Cosmetology

Especially in recent years, the business of beauty care has begun to contribute a heavy rain of chemicals to the environment. Sprays, soaps, powders, ointments, lotions, and other chemicals are being used in greater and greater amounts. The result is a multimillion-dollar paradox: beauty care contributes to the degradation of the environment. Man is seriously degrading the environment that gave him his sense of beauty in the first place.

In the studying of hairstyling and beauty care, a very careful look should be given to the contents of the various compounds used. How many have received adequate testing for toxicity to living organisms of all kinds? How much of each such chemical is daily released in a typical beauty shop? Special attention should also be given to use of electric power and water. How much electricity goes into the maintenance of fashion styles that did not go into beauty before the industrial era? What volumes of water are used, both in the shop and in the manufacture of the various substances used in beauty care?

Perhaps a cosmetology class can work out a "least energy and chemical" treatment that can be offered on a practice basis, then suggested to local hairdressers. A customer might then be presented an opportunity to compromise her own with the environment's beauty. It might be pointed out that the bargain is not only a cheaper treatment, but that it helps ensure that another generation will have the chance to know what beauty is.

Driver Education

What is said above about auto shop is applicable to driver education. The responsibilities involved in training new drivers are just as great as those involved in teaching future mechanics. The problem of transportation by means of personal vehicle cannot be left uninvestigated. An excellent project for a driver education class would be to monitor the amount and kind of pollutants emitted during test drives. Concurrently another group could experiment, perhaps with help from a biology class, in measuring the effects of such pollutants on plants and other organisms.

A lesson that ought to be incorporated into the basic methods of driving a car is that a car is a last resort. Only if you can find no better way to travel should a car be used. It might be pointed out that people who cannot afford the gasoline and people that live far from trading outlets must save their trips. They only travel when there is a maximum number of purchases or activities to be accomplished. The development of localized shopping centers, instead of leading to the development of foot and bicycle travel, seems to have given people an excuse to travel for the most minimal distances and reasons. Suggestions on how to budget the use of a car should be a part of every driver education class.

Driver education is the best of all situations in which to initiate regular units of walker education. After initial test drives, the class can be led on a walk through some of the same areas. The number of details noticed on the walk, the absence of noise, and the number of pollutants not released can then be compared to the advantages of the car trip: speed and carrying capacity. Driver education offers a rich field for innovation. It should not be presented without some extensive consideration of the environmental effects of driving, perhaps the most damaging of all man's present habits.

Drug Education

Whether any kind of drug education offered in schools is or can be successful is not for this book to say. In a drug program, however, consideration of and involvement with environment may make some very useful contributions. The senses in which drug problems are environmental problems are important.

The expanding awareness lure of drugs has everything to do with the environment. To expand awareness certainly is not the only reason drugs are used. Many initial uses, however, are made for perceptual kicks. Contributing to the need for such perceptual adventures are at least two environmental problems. One is the comparative sterility of urban or suburban environments. Admittedly, the concentration of human individuals in such areas provides much greater opportunity and even necessity for human contacts than in rural or wild situations. But man lives neither by bread alone nor by human contact alone. Humans, in spite of their complex variety, are nevertheless of a kind. The concentration of them into our metropolitan areas has developed in such a way as to exclude other animate and inanimate kinds. The experimental richness provided by contact with other species of animals and plants is largely denied the metropolitan dweller in his daily existence.

Financially and temporally there is a limited amount that the school can do to offset the grayness of a student's experience. Schools may already be providing the major amount of experiential variety in some students' lives. Field trips out of the local area, striving for as much environmental diversity as possible, should be increased. Microenvironments kept within the school for student observation should be expanded. Field trips to diverse, less institutionalized (wild, if possible) areas may do much to stimulate exercise of perceptual skills and to indicate the choices of habitats that are available for living things, including man.

Whether or not field trips and exposure to different environments are even possible for a school, however, the most effective means of preventing perceptual atrophy are available to all schools. The shifts that can be made in all classes at all levels toward greater reliance on nonverbal awareness, communication, and understanding will have the greatest effects on the students' perceptual environment. These have been discussed under several sections above. Their importance is underscored by the turning to drugs.

The second environment-drug relationship has to do with time and pace. So much can be learned about environment, self, and other individuals by taking the time to do nothing but be aware. Simply to listen, without comment, movement, self-distraction, or later discussion can be the most informative of experiences. Yet how often are students or teachers given the opportunity to see where they are in a school day, or even a year? One can learn, in such an attitude, what one has in the way of perceptual ability, and what one can do to be aware on a more regularly penetrating basis. Chemicals that aid this penetration are far less inviting when one has found ways of becoming aware and of continually developing his own awareness. Respect for the inborn capacity for awareness increases as awareness is allowed to grow.

If our society was such that time for awareness was commonly provided by other institutions or customarily taken by individuals on their own, the school would have a less important role to play (and environmental imbalance would probably be significantly less). But the time, even the suggestion to take the time, is extremely rare in our society. Somehow the cartoon show, the comic book, the evening news, the math assignment, the phone call, the model plane . . . something is always there to occupy us and to keep our noses to the busy ground of living. A significant aspect of drug experiences and a prime contributor to drugs' success in enhancing awareness is that, under drug effects or under the excuse of drug effects, time is taken to do nothing but perceive. Without the drug, if time is taken for the same purpose of centering one's self on perception or on introspection (if they can be so classified), equally worthwhile experience can come, greater growth can be stimulated.

Environmental ironies are getting to be a dime a dozen. An especially important one, however, centers on this problem of awareness. We, who both pride and condemn ourselves for the unprecedented use we make of the environment, turn that use to insulating ourselves further and further from the most pleasing of uses, awareness. There is joy in awareness, in interaction with the aesthetics of the environment; we cut ourselves off from that joy with every convenience that mechanically intervenes between us and environment. The internal-combustion engine is certainly as addicting as any drug and may stimulate suicidal hallucinations of grandeur. Environmental problems must above all suggest to those involved in drug education that the drug problems they are dealing with deserve great sympathy and respect. The ultimate solution is not the elimination of the search for kicks. The search for kicks, in fact, provides the ultimate lesson: convenience is worthless without joy. An environment less dominated by man can be a joy and can expand man's mind. The young users of drugs may only be giving the signs of the first famine, their minds starved by convenience.

Government

The study of the role and duties of the American citizen and of governments in general is crucial to development of competence in dealing with environmental problems. How can people concerned about environmental conditions effectively express and exercise their commitment to a healthy world? What are the inherent problems of separate nation-state governments in the quest for environmental balance? A government class can work out and experiment with model national goals and foreign policies to estimate their effects upon the world environment.

The environment knows no bounds. Its own all-inclusive territory takes precedence over man's recent political parceling. To manage one population's interaction with resources and cycles, then, is ultimately unsuccessful without the cooperation of all populations. Within the United States, where we must hope that governmental solutions to environmental problems can be forthcoming, the proper focus would seem to be on the need for regional government. Where our traditional state, county, city structure proves most inefficient is in its dealing with environmental conditions. Models must be worked out, and some few are presently being tried, to align jurisdictions along environmentally sound borders. A government class can take up the local watershed or atmospheric region and try to evaluate the environmental rationality of current governmental organization. The boundaries of the states themselves, important as they may have been in the past, impede environmentally sound action in many cases. While states are changeable conceptions in the minds and on the papers of men, environmental processes can submit to far less alteration.

The study of the environmental significance of public documents is of the greatest interest. What notions of the finiteness of this country can be deduced from reading the Constitution or Declaration of Independence? According to those documents, just what is the environment of the United States? Is environment private property, public property? Is freedom, as described in the country's founding documents, predicated upon some particular environmental condition? What key notions in the Constitution and amendments appear to conflict with environmental principles?

Citizenship in environment is even more laden with responsibility than citizenship in the nation. Each offers rights only after the assumption of proper duties. Just as he who claims he is denied the rights of citizenship in the nation must look to his own involvement before expecting satisfaction, he who claims he is denied the clean environment to which he is entitled should look first to the amount of contamination for which he is responsible. A government class can consider what duties must be undertaken by those who claim the right of environmental health.

The consumer who is or who believes that he is dependent upon a particular product presents a great problem in environmental citizenship. The product, as are many products these days, may not be environmentally sound. It may contribute wastes or drain resources to an unacceptable degree. A government class can play the roles of concerned consumer, concerned middleman, concerned manufacturer, and concerned regulatory agency to get at the chicken-and-egg connections that make reduction of environmental imbalance exceedingly difficult no matter how sincere the concern.

The greatest problem in government and citizenship is the long-standing problem of participation itself. An active democracy could be the best of all governments for maintenance of environmental balance. The input from the participating members might approach the coverage needed to monitor environmental conditions; the self-government of individuals might accomplish the variety of interactions needed to maintain balanced conditions. But an inactive democracy may be yet worse for the environment than a dictatorship. Citizens are the feedback link between environment and government. Blocking either input or output through their own inertia, a people can make environmental interaction far too clumsy to be successful. The relatively more direct connection attainable in a dictatorship may allow somewhat more effective action.

Population size, after a point, seriously inhibits individually responsible activity. The feeling of any sort of community of the United States is strained to the limits. It is both held intact and threatened daily by the electronic communications network, particularly television. A government class can consider the potential futures of the United States. Will participation in government, will even voting attendance increase with increasing population? Would 300 million Americans be more responsible and responsive than 200 million? Or would this democracy function better at 100 million? If so, might not incentives for limited families, often seen as dictatorial measures, be steps toward a less dictatorial and more viable democracy? Is a nation founded ultimately to grow or to endure?

Health

Health courses have often provided the most extensive formal coverage of environmental problems in a student's education. It is impossible meaningfully to cover personal health without considering the health of the environment. In health courses as in others, however, conceptions of environment have stopped too short. There is room for a much greater contribution to environmental understanding in the study of health.

An individual of any species can be no healthier, ultimately, than the environment. It would be interesting for a health class to explore how man has partly realized this and acted to ensure local environmental health, but has failed to realize that local health is impossible to maintain. We easily learn that our own garbage cannot be kept in our own houses. We are slower to learn, however, that it cannot simply be dumped outside. Is there any realization among members of the health class or among those planning the local sanitation system that too much garbage or sewage, whether treated or untreated, cannot be kept in a balanced world? The living Earth depends upon a moderate amount of nutrient organic matter. As man digs further into Earth's resources he creates an overload of organic waste that unbalances the world. There is no keeping house in such an unbalanced world.

We know that many diseases are infestations of our bodies by some other organism. Disease is often nothing more than an extreme or unbalanced form of coexistence, with one animal's or plant's substance being turned into raw material for another. Another concept important to the study of health is that the role of disease agent is by no means restricted to any group of organisms. All organisms, if unrestrained by others, act as diseases on the environment's living and nonliving resources. It would be worthwhile for a health class to consider man from this viewpoint.

An investigation may clarify this view of man. Students can be asked to contribute one day's worth of their family's garbage, the remnants of three meals and the day's other activities. Only a couple of volunteers are needed to bring in their collections. Other students could make a tally at home without actually exhibiting the materials in class. Certainly some care should be taken regarding sanitation in class; in fact this investigation might best be pursued outside. However it is carried out, the object is to weigh, measure, and count the amounts of various materials in a typical day's garbage. Depending upon the family's size, multiply by some representative proportion of the world's 3½ billion population. Then, considering the sources and amounts of the materials turned to human use and discarded, ask whether man is acting as a disease organism.

Finally, it should be made clear in a health class that

the health of a human individual is now directly related to the health of the human species. An experiment in contagion is never difficult to run in a public school. As a disease spreads through students and teachers the opportunity for acquiring absentee figures should be taken as the basis for an examination of man's overall health. The combination of transportation and dense centers of population, human monocultures, has made the spread of disease among humans all the more likely in spite of advances in health protection. In an urban area in particular a continuing study could be made of the frequency and extent of disease waves passing through the school each year. Are the advances in health science, medicine, and civil engineering keeping up with the advances in population and population concentration? If the industrialized world's high level of nutrition is maintained at the expense of the underdeveloped world, the susceptibility of both to epidemic diseases will continue to increase. The underdeveloped countries become more vulnerable as their nutrition remains inadequate; the industrialized countries become more vulnerable through their contacts with the underdeveloped majorities. A health class could perhaps answer the question: Is it healthy to have a great deal more, in the way of food and energy, than all your neighbors? Health might be said to be sharing among organisms; might it not then require sharing among human beings?

Home Economics

The New York State School of Home Economics at Cornell University was recently renamed the "School of Human Ecology." If this name change catches on, home economics may have just as good a mandate to take a holistic approach to the environment as Earth science now does. That home is the beginning of environment for a family, just as the classroom is the beginning for a class, should be clear.

All the environmental inventories and evaluations discussed in the chapters on the classroom, school, and district are certainly applicable to the home. After carrying out such inventories either in the home economics classroom or in students' own homes, perhaps the following question should be pursued: Do any other animals impound so much of Earth's resources and energy in the maintenance of their own dwellings? A further question: Does a family necessarily have to pursue a course of economic expansion throughout its life, using more and more power and materials to the limit of its buying power? Might not a family lead at least as humane an existence by trying each year to use a bit less than the year before: to walk oftener than ride; to wear less variety of clothes; to rely less on electric light; to reuse any container purchased for its contents; to use fewer chemicals for cleaning, spraying, waxing, painting; to spend less and less time with machines, more time with noninstitutional, nonindustrial environmental interaction?

In studying nutrition, students should have the opportunity to compare nutritional quality and quantity for the world's peoples. It is less and less tolerable for the well-fed people to be ignorant of the nutritional gap between them and their neighbors, some of them their own countrymen. Concurrently, the study of foods should not leave out an investigation of the environments that supply their nutritive content. Particularly interesting, for example, is the importation of protein sources to well-developed countries from countries that are suffering severe protein shortages. The rich variety of foods to which we have become accustomed may well be drastically reduced as the developing countries seek to feed themselves.

Whenever particular products are used in the home economics classroom they should be subject to as deep as possible an investigation into their environmental significance. Where have they come from? What are their effects within the household in which they are used? And where are they bound after use? The homemaker is subject to perhaps the greatest of all advertising barrages in order to increase and complexify her use of materials and resources. A home economics class is an excellent forum for comparison of the benefits attained by such overuse to the environmental damage done.

This brings us to the central relationship of home economics to environment. To paraphrase Thoreau, no home is of any value without "a tolerable planet" to live on. Cleanliness, convenience, efficiency, even harmony within a home is of little use if it is obtained at the expense of the harmony of the living Earth. There is no way to insulate a home from the environment out of which it is made. Perhaps a home economics class ought to spend as much time as a class in natural history on field trips to observe the homes of our fellow animals.

Physical Education

Physical activity is interaction with environment. No course could be more dependent on a healthy environment than physical education. Dramatic illustrations of this are readily available in smog-ridden cities that have curtailed athletic activities in their schools on many days throughout the year.

The irony of the human situation is again apparent when considering physical activity. In days of less convenience and fewer conveniences, physical exertion was a more integrated part of living. Conveniences have made physical education necessary. Exercise must be engaged in for its own sake. Yet many of the same leisure-giving conveniences are rapidly fouling the environment, making physical exertion even hazardous to health. Again, environmental health and individual health are inseparable.

Perhaps physical education can become a study in which we rediscover ways of integrating physical activity into daily life. A class in P.E. could investigate the time-saving but activity-preventing roles of various devices and appliances. How could individual exercise accomplish the same task, perhaps losing a bit of time, and eliminate the need for the machinery, fuel, and materials? Walking, rather than riding, is an obvious activity to begin with.

Whatever maintenance is required on the physical education department's equipment and grounds, and perhaps even on the entire school's grounds, should be attempted on this environment-saving rather than time-saving basis. Are power mowers needed for the lawns, or can exercise be gained through their cutting? Do plastics have to be used, or can nonsynthetic materials be maintained to serve the same purposes? Does weeding require a herbicide, or can a bit of pulling accomplish the same?

Any power equipment used by an athletic department should receive very careful consideration. If new lights are contemplated for the field, to make night games possible, will they be worth it? For they will contribute to the demand on the generating plant, which fouls the air with pollutants that make day or night games less and less possible to play? Can an electric scoreboard be replaced with cards and a little teamwork on the sidelines?

Physical education and athletic contests are popular because, essentially, environmental interaction is a joyful, strengthening, and positive activity. In his love for exercise and the contest may lie man's saving emotion, out of which he may see the environmental bill of goods he has sold himself for what it is: a complication of environmentally damaging devices that insulate him from the very world with which he is built to interact. The range of exercises that man can accomplish, swinging, running, swimming, tumbling, is an unmistakable gift from his background of varied environments: forest, savanna, lake, lowland, highland. For us to remain truly human we must preserve those environments that challenge the potentials they once molded in us.

Sex Education

Sex education, whether institutional or private, must take into special account one central relationship of sex to environment. Without environmental diversity, sexual reproduction, with all its attendant risks, pleasures, and pains, would never have been likely to evolve. If the world had remained a uniform organic soup, as some imagine it was some billions of years ago, there would never have been a premium on flexibility of genetic adaptation, which is the principal biological contribution of sexual reproduction. The necessity to play the game of genetic chance to produce offspring is also the opportunity to mix and remix gene combinations that might never occur in the template-after-template-after-template reproduction of cellular fission.

The proponents of test-tube reproduction, who would replace this adaptational roulette with their own conception of accuracy and perfection, are served well by the deterioration of Earth's habitats. A uniformly humanized world, in which all habitats have been made to resemble a single ideal, has no need of the sexual game. Again we find that the health of the environment, in this case its diversity, is directly connected to the happiness of one of its parts, mankind.

Sexual attraction and intercourse have come to mean more to the human animal than the simple production of offspring. Nonetheless, the "more" that we have come to call love is no less dependent upon the environmental variety and space that gave rise to sexual reproduction in the first place. Nowhere is the tragedy of the commons more evident, nowhere is it more a real tragedy: the love that might give rise to a host of children is made less and less accessible to those children if indeed they are a host. The tragedy is increasingly visited upon our offspring, if we give the Earth too many of them.

We can probably never return to the environmental edge at which our reproductive capacity was fully justified because of the hazards to which we were subjected. What we can do, if indeed we are capable of both foresight and love, is establish a stable population well back from the possible carrying capacity of our environment. Perhaps we can increase our own carrying capacity for love if we give ourselves the environmental room.

Though there is undoubtedly some place for study of population curves and dynamics in sex education, the facts and figures are themselves sterile. More important is the consideration of the love emotion that the environment, through sex, has given man. Is it possible, for instance, to love another in a truly silent spring?

Shop

Shop is a primary user of energy and materials. Both of these should be treated as environment much as the artist and writer should treat their materials. If at all possible, the class should be able to observe the source of the materials in forests and mines. An inventory of all the attendant materials and energy that go into the final manufacture of the wood or metal should be included in the introduction to the materials themselves.

The increasing use of power tools raises serious questions. How much energy is being used, and from what sources, to power the tools? What operations can be done by hand without the aid of extra power? Is the environmental drain worth it in any given case? The class can experiment with some individuals attempting to turn out equivalent pieces without aid of power while others use the power tools.

A shop class can lead an investigation and experiment in material reuse. Scrap woods and metals gathered by the class, or reused materials purchased from a recycling plant, can be compared with new materials for the construction of various projects.

Ultimately a shop class concerning itself with environment can make a great contribution by demonstrating how useful objects can be made from simple materials without a great deal of energy other than thoroughly biodegradable human exertion. The competence learned by practicing a craft with one's own two hands can go far in reconnecting an individual to his environment. The shroud of industrial processes that hides an individual's effect on environment by intervening between resource and user can be at least partly removed by building for oneself.

Chapter Four

Interdisciplinary Study

I am writing this in a forest camp in New York State. A group of people are gathered here to learn about the environment, its principles, present status, and potentials. We call our endeavor an ecology course, an attempt to learn general ecology through field experience in the forest. But just what is the range of our subject matter?

This forest cannot be understood without the aid of the biological sciences: we must know something of the properties of specific living organisms, of the processes of evolutionary adaptation, of the general requirements for life. It cannot be understood without the physical sciences: we must know something of the chemistry of waters and soils, something of the thermodynamics of the atmosphere. We can neither measure nor communicate many forest properties without mathematics.

The forest cannot be understood without the help of history: the time and the nature of European habitation or use of the forest has seriously affected its present character. The present state of the forest cannot be understood without knowledge of government: all manner of laws, restrictions, and political boundaries affect even our access to the forest. We must know some anthropology to understand the environment we see: American Indian customs seriously affected the ecology of this area before European settlement.

Interdisciplinary Study

To understand both the present state and the future possibilities of the forest environment we must know both past and present economics: certain trees would not be here but for economically justified neglect. Many stands are presently managed for economic purposes. To place values on environmental quality we refer back to the senses and interpretations of the literary and graphic artists. The animals we find are not neutral, but are transformed by our imaginations working with artists' imagery.

To explain public use of the forest and to explain many of our own reactions, we rely on psychology: many deer survive in this particular stand because of the social habits of deer hunters. To communicate our understanding of the forest among ourselves and to others we must constantly define and redefine words and establish word usages. To understand the detergent suds in the streams we must know something of the applications being made upstream of chemicals in various agricultural and industrial processes. As we travel in automobiles we must understand how our own boisterous presence affects the forest that we see and must weigh the advantages of such transportation against the disadvantages of limiting and injuring our object of study.

In short, the environment is an interdisciplinary reality requiring interdisciplinary study. No single subject area could cover the forest, or any other environment, without having to reach often into other areas of knowledge. We are, in fact, limited by the success with which we can integrate the contributions made by the various studies of the environment. The success of environmental education in large measure depends upon the success with which it can integrate disciplines. Our thought has developed and still largely operates in a discontinuous field of categories. To understand and to apply successfully the principles of the Earth environment, we must succeed in developing the connections between these categories.

Environmental education's dependence on interdisciplinary study should not be taken to imply a need for a sudden generalization of curricular areas. An attempt to produce solely general environmental education would most probably result in the cultivation of incompetence. Neither can we expect to succeed in developing some sort of specialty in environmental omniscience. Ecology's most important lesson may well be to have shown us just how far from omniscience we are. But we can educate to fill in the gaps of our compartmentalized approach to environment.

There are a few encouraging signs that an interdisciplinary approach has been recognized and is being considered fundamental to environmental education. The Earth Science Curriculum Project has taken an avowedly interdisciplinary approach in preparing its basic materials. ESCP's recent inner-city environmental studies efforts, described in part three, chapter one, represent a challenging application of interdisciplinary thinking. The Biological Sciences Curriculum Study has just embarked on a joint curriculum project with social science teachers. The results of the initial writing conferences of biology and social studies teachers should be well worth attention. *People and Their Environment,* "Teachers' Curriculum Guides to Conservation Education," developed in South Carolina, is an admirable set of suggestions about the relationships of conservation to the various traditional subject areas. Used creatively, these guides can stimulate important communication between the subjects and grades covered. The key to successful interdisciplinary education does not lie in use of such curriculum packages, however. No matter how good, packages remain packages and suggest static relationships not found in the environment.

Alteration of the structure of department and subject divisions within the school can make possible real interdisciplinary education. As always, the best offerings in a school will be made by teachers who have developed their own programs out of their own and their students' interests. In the case of interdisciplinary study the best offerings will come from the cooperative efforts of such teachers from different subject specialties. Restructuring of the school can greatly assist and stimulate such cooperation.

A method currently being tried at the John Adams High

School in Portland, Oregon, and perhaps in other schools, is the house system of general education. The student body is more or less randomly divided into groups, each group becoming the members of a house working with a group of teachers, perhaps one each in math, science, social science, and English. These teachers, working with their house and with an overseeing curriculum advisor, plan a coordinated general education which they pursue during half the normal school day. The focus of the house may be jointly agreed upon, and the offerings in each subject area may then be coordinated to sharpen and develop that focus.

With half the school day for their efforts, time can be much more effectively distributed for all members of the house, students and faculty alike. There is no need to follow the rigid daily schedule of fifty-minute classes. Instead of this artificial structure, a structure based upon the study itself can be followed by the house. The web of relationships studied in this manner more nearly represents the operation of the environment than does the traditionally pigeonholed schedule of subjects.

There are goals for such a house system, or for any other attempt at interdisciplinary education, that can especially contribute to environmental education. As great an emphasis can be placed on the interactions between disciplines as upon the content of the disciplines themselves. Environmentally the most interesting information for study, usually the most neglected information as well, concerns the effects of social phenomena on biological, or values on actual practices, or practices-on-biological-phenomena-on-values. These interfaces deserve at least as much attention as the main bodies of the subject areas.

Also, though the easiest and most often studied connections between subjects occur among the members of one group, such as the observers, perhaps the most important connections occur between subjects in different groups. The values communicated and developed in the interpreter disciplines have great need of interaction with the findings of the observers. Both interpreters and observers need close study with the practicing disciplines of the users. Thus, while a social science-natural science interaction is certainly valuable, at least as valuable would be the interdisciplinary effort between a science and an art, or between either of these and some practical skill. General science and English, for instance, have much to learn of their effects on each other. History can profitably coordinate with a shop class. Earth science, literature, and sex education have much to contribute to each other.

Environmental education and education in general will be best served if interdisciplinary offerings are built in each school on the basis of teachers' interests and compatibility. Teachers who can work together should work together; out of their cooperation can come education beyond the level of any curricular development, no matter how sophisticated. If interdisciplinary development can occur among compatible teachers, if these teachers can concentrate on the interaction between observation, values, and practices, and if the school can be used as its own best environmental model, environmental education will have taken a great stride forward.

Conclusion

Teaching for Survival

As I complete the writing of this book, I am reminded by a statement in the July 24, 1970, *Life* that my title is inadequate. René Dubos writes in that issue that "mere survival is not enough." Of course he is correct. Survival is neither enough nor is it really man's problem. Adaptability has been man's hallmark, distinguishing him from his fellow organisms. His genetic makeup is such that his behavioral capacities are unusually diverse. This has allowed him to be not so immediately dependent upon a quality environment for his survival as are other animals.

Yet that which we call most human about us is every bit as dependent upon environmental quality as it was when we endured the ice ages. This is the part of man that leads Dubos and others to conclude that mere survival, as a goal, can only lead to our survival as "something less than human." We have taught ourselves for generations that we are different from the animals in our possession of a soul, something within us that valued, cared, and expressed emotion. Similarly we have taught ourselves that we are animals, comparable in all manner of ways to other organisms. It is time that we took both of these teachings seriously. The animal and his soul are inseparable. Humanness is the sum of these two that is greater than either taken separately.

Last night the aurora borealis painted itself over this forest. Not engineered, timed, directed, or produced by man, the distant streaks had no more regularity of form, either in space or in time, than the star background against which they played. Yet in their randomness and in their unannounced coming and going these northern lights had the capacity to draw cries of amazement and appreciation from our small huddle of temporary forest residents. We ran to turn off lights or cover them to give the sky a fair chance to show itself; we chattered, pointed, sometimes fell silent, and somehow were refreshed. If we had left on the lights we rushed to extinguish, if we had not bothered to look twice in the night sky, or if we now tolerate the fouling of the atmosphere by our own polluting engines so that we may never again see the aurora, we would be less than human. Survival without the aurora borealis would not be enough.

I taught a small class in biology this past year. From the standpoint of skin color we were a motley group, gathering our own spectrum of pigments together for the last period of every school day. From the standpoint of ethnic backgrounds we were even more diverse. Indeed, there was little rhyme or reason to our group, even as small as it was, even though all but one of us were high-school sophomores from a small town. Somehow we had the capacity to draw cries of amazement and appreciation from each other, as well as laughter, anger, and occasional boredom. We talked, observed, created, sometimes fell silent, and somehow, even through the trial of a much-despised final exam, were refreshed by our year together. If we did not now bother to hail each other on the street, or if we tolerated the exclusion of any of our group because of color, background, or economics, we would be less than human. Survival without human diversity would not be enough.

Both these experiences required standards of environmental quality. Too much atmospheric pollution, on the one hand, or the pressure of population to the exclusion of an ethnic group on the other, would have made the aurora or the biology class impossible. There are those cities where the aurora can no longer be seen. There are certainly similar cities where the pressure to exclude a human group is great. In both places the level of existence is that much nearer to mere survival.

Perhaps this book should have been titled *Teaching for Coexistence,* if that were not such an unwieldy phrase. For somehow we must learn how to coexist with the aurora and with men of different colors. We cannot coexist with the aurora without being careful of the atmosphere; we cannot coexist with each other without stopping to listen. In either case we need room. Crowded together in a metropolis we cannot see the aurora; crowded together in a classroom we have not the time to listen. Crowded together on this planet we can be no more human than ants crowded into their colonies. The successful ants show us that such survival is possible, but they do not show us how to be human.

In part one, chapter one, I mentioned that I suspected environment could not be taught without teaching humanity and vice versa. Surely this is true. Humanity cannot exist without quality environment. Humanity can be measured against man's treatment of the nonhuman world. Respect for one's fellows, for environment, and for posterity must be one. None of these can be meaningful without the operation of the others. This is one reason why a straight ecology course can never, in isolation, accomplish environmental education of the kind called for in this book. The humaneness of the school environment itself must be constructively maintained.

Many objections are raised, particularly by those who have been concerned with environmental quality for years and who have been dealing with the practical problems of its maintenance, against environmental emotionalism. The surge of press coverage, books, citizens' groups, and accompanying rhetoric is highly charged with emotion. The connotations taken on by words once the property of pure and applied scientists have made these words seem tarnished and less useful to such environmental practitioners. "Environment," "pollution," and "ecology" are the most obvious examples. Yet, with all due respect to those who raise such objections, what may well save us from further environmental degradation is emotion itself.

Emotion ought to be distinguished from hysteria, which is emotion come loose at the seams. Our notions of humanity and, correspondingly, of environment are not neutral. They are value-laden. These values and their expression through emotion are inseparable. We only recognize our values by emotion. Pure ecology can tell us how environmental systems work, how one animal may grow in population size only at the expense of another, for instance. But, other than saying "Systems are nice to work with," ecology cannot assign values. Ecologists objecting to this statement will find, at the root of the values they espouse, emotions.

Hysterical reaction to environmental crises is to be avoided as far as is possible. But emotion, supporting an environmental value, is the stuff with which humanity must survive in order to remain human. Ecological principles can inform emotion, and values must be tempered against our scientific understanding of the environment. But to intend to remain neutral or emotionless in a study of the environment is a frustrating and dehumanizing task. Environmental action must be based on the development of new values or in the refining of expression of old ones. Ultimately, our caring about the environment is all that can move us to bear our environmental responsibilities more wisely.

It is well to repeat here a caution against indoctrination. Many plans "to require the environment" and to instill in the hearts and minds of students environmental values are either blatant plans for indoctrination or such by implication. Indoctrination is the educational equivalent of hysterical reaction. Let us hope that students are close enough to their environments to see through such one-sided attempts to drill them in an environmental education. Human values and environmental values must ultimately be one. To force the latter down anyone's throat is to neglect criminally one of the most important of the former: freedom of thought. To settle for indoctrination tactics in environmental education is to work against environmental quality. Surviving at the expense of intellectual

Conclusion

freedom would be no better than surviving at the expense of the aurora borealis or of human diversity.

In conclusion I would like to pass on the thoughts of Liberty Hyde Bailey, one of the foremost philosophers of environmental education, writing in 1903. This section from his book *The Nature-Study Idea* was written in the environmental terminology of his own era, when the pressures were not so great: world population was approximately 1½ billion and was not to double for some sixty years. Read in the light of today's environmental predicament, Bailey's words can still inform us and give us hope:

Nature-study is not science. It is not knowledge. It is not facts. It is spirit. It is concerned with the child's outlook on the world.

Nature-study will endure, because it is natural and of universal application. Methods will change and will fall into disrepute; its name will be dropped from curriculums; here and there it will be encased in the schoolmaster's "method" and its life will be smothered; now and then it will be overexploited; with many persons it will be a fad; but the spirit will live . . .

It is one of the marks of the evolution of the race that we are coming more and more into sympathy with the objects of the external world. These things are a part of our lives. They are central to our thoughts. The happiest life has the greatest number of points of contact with the world, and it has the deepest feeling and sympathy for everything that is . . .

As yet there are no codified methods of teaching nature-study. The subject is not a formal part of the curriculum; and thereby it is not perfunctory. And herein lies much of its value—in the fact that it cannot be reduced to a system, is not cut and dried, cannot become a part of rigid school methods. Its very essence is spirit. It is as free as its subject-matter . . .

Bibliography

Introduction: The Need For Environmental Education

American Association of School Administrators	*Imperatives in Education,* Washington, D. C.: American Association of School Administrators, 1966
Bottomly, Forbes	"A Meaning to Our Work: One Administrator's View of Environmental Education," *Washington Education* 81 (May 1970) p. 40–41
Hammersley, A., E. Jones, and G. A. Perry	*Approaches to Environmental Studies,* London: Blandford Press, 1968
Hurd, Paul DeHart	*Biological Education in American Secondary Schools 1890–1960,* Washington, D. C.: American Institute of Biological Sciences, 1961
Johnson, Huey D., ed.	*No Deposit—No Return.* Reading, Mass.: Addison—Wesley, 1970.

Of all these books, the most interesting is the one by Hammersley, Jones, and Perry. It is intended as a handbook for environmental education methods and therefore might seem to belong to the "Environmental Education" category in this bibliography. It is of most interest not as a handbook, however, but as a case study in the problems of developing environmental education. The authors have put together an extensive collection of ideas that consistently fall short of the significant relationships of environment to education. It is a guide to study of the environment as an external object of academic interest. All this in spite of the fact that the introduction claims environmental education is the key to making education relevant. Unfortunately, extension of the purely academic view outside the classroom, with never a look back to the relationships connecting individual through classroom to outside environment, contributes little to environmental education.

Imperatives in Education, quoted in the text, also provides an insight into the problems of environmental education. The section on wise use of natural resources, from which the quotation was taken, shows an admirable interest in environmental problems but, again, a lack of understanding of basic relationships between environment and education.

Hurd's book is an invaluable collection of the proceedings of major science and life science curriculum meetings over a seventy-year period. It is interesting to watch how long our intentions have been good, our proclamations have been published, yet our habits have gone unchanged in environmental education.

Major sections of Dr. Bottomly's article are quoted in the text. The entire issue of *Washington Education* cited is devoted to environmental education and is well worth attention.

No Deposit—No Return is an anthology of papers presented at the 13th National Conference of the U. S. National Commission for UNESCO, held November 1969 in San Francisco. Besides being an interesting collection of diverse readings, the book contains some valuable philosophy and proposals for environmental education in papers presented by Michael Scriven, Paul DeHart Hurd, and Sterling Bunnell.

The Abundance of Environmental Educators (I-1)

Divoky, Diane, ed.	*How Old Will You Be in 1984?* New York: Avon, 1969
Lewis, C. S.	*The Abolition of Man,* New York: Crowell-Collier, 1947
Rosenthal, Robert, and Lenore Jacobson	*Pygmalion in the Classroom,* New York: Holt, Rinehart & Winston, 1968

How Old Will You Be in 1984? is a collection of articles from high-school "underground" newspapers. For secondary-school teachers in particular, this book may be the most important discussion of education available. Effects of various classroom and school environments, as they reflect the "outside" environment, are evident in each of the student writings.

Lewis's book, though more than twenty years old and aimed at English schools, still provides a penetrating look at the effects of typical textbooks on a student's idea of nature. The title essay is also an excellent critical review of the idea that man has "conquered" nature.

Pygmalion in the Classroom is a report of a study of the effect of teacher expectations on student performance. Read with "environment" in mind, it demonstrates the degree to which the dominant force in most classroom environments is, simply, the teacher.

Overuse and Overgrowth (I-2)

Ehrenfeld, David W.	*Biological Conservation*, New York: Holt, Rinehart & Winston, 1970
Kormondy, Edward J.	*Concepts of Ecology*, Englewood Cliffs, N. J.: Prentice-Hall, 1968
Odum, Eugene P.	*Ecology*, New York: Holt, Rinehart & Winston, 1963

Each of these is available as a relatively inexpensive paperback. They comprise short, well-illustrated, and detailed introductions to the fundamentals of ecology. Ehrenfeld's book elaborates on the question of man's effects and management on ecosystems and is probably best preceded by a reading of either of the other volumes. Valuable as introductions, these books also put ecology into the perspective of its limitations.

Borgstrom, Georg	*Too Many*, Toronto: Collier-Macmillan, 1969
Committee on Resources and Man	*Resources and Man*, San Francisco: Freeman, 1969
Dorst, Jean	*Before Nature Dies*, Boston: Houghton Mifflin, 1970
Ehrlich, Paul R., and Anne H. Ehrlich	*Population Resources Environment*, San Francisco: W. H. Freeman, 1970
Hardin, Garrett, ed.	*Population, Evolution, and Birth Control*, San Francisco: W. H. Freeman, 1969

Nicholson, Max	*The Environmental Revolution,* New York: McGraw-Hill, 1970
Young, Louise B., ed.	*Population in Perspective,* New York: Oxford University Press, 1968
Ziswiler, Vinzenz	*Extinct and Vanishing Animals,* New York: Springer-Verlag, 1967.

The Ehrlichs' work stands now as the most comprehensive survey of man's ecological problems.

Resources and Man contains articles contributed by members of the Committee on Resources of Man of the National Resources Council and the National Academy of Science. A summary of man's position in the biosphere is provided by Marston Bates; particular materials and energy sources are considered separately.

Borgstrom's *Too Many* is subtitled *A Study of Earth's Biological Limitations.* The author is a leader in the field of food science, and this work is particularly valuable for its consideration of water, soil, and food.

Both Hardin's and Young's collections of readings on population are excellent. Each covers a wide variety of commentators from ancient times and other cultures to present Western man.

Nicholson and Dorst present British and European perspectives on the growth of an environmental sense, of active conservation efforts, and of worldwide conservation problems.

Ziswiler's short work considers the complex factors in human behavior that lead to the extinction of our fellow animals, and summarizes the extent of these irretrievable losses.

Audubon	1130 Fifth Ave., New York, N. Y. 10028 ($8.50/yr.)
Catalyst for Environmental Quality	Circulation Dept., 274 Madison Ave., New York, N. Y. 10016 ($5/yr. quarterly)
Environment	438 N. Skinker Blvd., St. Louis, Mo. 63130 ($8.50/yr.)
Environment Action Bulletin	Rodale Press, Emmaus, Pa. 18049 ($10/yr. weekly)

Intecol Bulletin	Secretary General, Intecol, c/o Institute of Biology, 41 Queen's Gate, London, S.W. 7, England
Natural History	American Museum of Natural History, Central Park West at 79th St., New York, N. Y. 10024 ($7/yr.)
Saturday Review	380 Madison Ave., New York, N. Y. 10017 ($10/yr.)

The job of "keeping up" with environmental actions and the state of the environment is a formidable one. Lately there has been a publishing revolution spawning new journals and renaming old ones. An early casualty of the lack of funds that threatens such new ventures was perhaps the most valuable of all the new contributions, *Earth Times*. Watch for any signs of its rebirth. In a well-edited newspaper format, it did a better job of covering environmental happenings in its first issues than any other periodical this author has seen.

The job of separating quality coverage from rhetoric has become about as difficult as keeping up with environmental events themselves. The periodicals listed above show promise of avoiding the pitfalls of rhetoric.

Environment Action Bulletin is probably the best classroom aid of those listed. It presents short digest articles on a weekly basis and is making a brave attempt to contribute and publish suggestions for practical application of environmental good sense. It also is carrying a growing list of state antipollution and other environmental organizations.

Saturday Review devotes every fourth issue to the environment, publishing important articles of philosophy concerning the interface between environment and human values. A world environmental watch and book reviews usually accompany the lead articles.

Catalyst publishes a few major articles of environmental philosophy, a few on specific environmental problems, and includes a section on classroom teaching aids, books, films, equipment, and projects.

Both *Audubon* and *Natural History* are providing better and better coverage of environmental problems, centering on threatened species or threatened habitats, but branching out considerably. For aesthetic values, *Audubon* provides relatively cheap access to some of the very finest photography of this Earth and its inhabitants.

Environment provides more technical coverage than any

of the above. Yet it is still a layman's magazine, sort of the *Scientific American* of environmental science.

Intecol Bulletin is a new international effort that will probably be at least as technical as *Environment*. It is in its formative stages, however, and is open to suggestions. The influence of letters and subscriptions from educators could bring its attention to the problems of environmental education.

Population Bulletin; *World Population* *Data Sheet*	Population Reference Bureau, 1755 Massachusetts Ave., NW, Washington, D. C. 20036 ($3/yr.)

For consideration of population problems there is no better resource than the Population Reference Bureau. The $3 rate is special to teachers and has been for years, though the resources of the bureau have been but slightly tapped.

The bureau, in cooperation with Maryland Planned Parenthood–World Population and the Carolina Population Center, hosted the first population education workshop held in this country in the spring of 1970. Some fifty teachers, primarily from secondary schools, came from all over the United States to begin pooling their own efforts with population education in various subject areas. Further conferences are planned, as well as publication of teaching aids.

Currently the annual subscription-membership fee brings six issues of the excellent *Population Bulletin,* unequaled in its field, and the *World Population Data Sheet,* a yearly wall chart of current demographic information about the countries of the world. In addition, another periodical entitled *People* is in the works, with special emphasis placed on education.

The bureau is eager to aid teachers in whatever ways seem necessary and invites inquiries and participation in coming conferences.

Time of Man	Ealing Corporation, 2225 Massachusetts Ave., Cambridge, Mass. 02140 (50 Minutes; rental $40/day; purchase $450)

As a teaching aid for secondary-school students, this movie stands out among all the rest. Produced with the resources of the American Museum of Natural History, it presents an integrated, informative, and arresting picture of man's position in the environment. Life-styles alternative to our own Western are presented, both successful and unsuccessful, both from other human populations and from populations of other living organisms.

The Classroom (II-1)

Harris, Frank W.	*Games,* Eastern Cooperative Recreation School, c/o Henry Brush, 1717 Hillside Road, Southhampton, Penna. 18966. ($2.00 per copy).
Kohl, Herbert R.	*36 Children,* New York: New American Library, 1967
Kohl, Herbert R.	*The Open Classroom,* New York: New York Review/Vintage, 1969
"Project Pointers Column"	*Science World,* 902 Sylvan Avenue, Englewood Cliffs, New Jersey 07632. ($1.75 per year—weekly.)
Romey, William D.	*Inquiry Techniques for Teaching Science,* Englewood Cliffs, N. J.: Prentice-Hall, 1968
Spolin, Viola	*Improvisation for the Theater,* Evanston, Ill., Northwestern University Press, 1963

Valuable insights into teachers' and students' minds have been provided by a number of very popular books in recent years. Of all these, those that have been most useful to me have been Herbert Kohl's. His *36 Children* has more of "children" in it than most books. It is most valuable for the relationship it shows between "humanity" and "environment." The values raised under the one banner cannot help but be applied to the other. *The Open Classroom* is a brief attempt to systematize some of the practical ideas that are implicit in the earlier work.

Romey's work, ostensibly for science teachers, can be read with great profit by teachers in general. With exercises, challenges, and evaluations for the teacher, the book provides a look at the classroom environment as it is affected by teacher behavior.

Improvisation for the Theater is the greatest hidden treasury of innovative teaching techniques for environmental education. It is a compendium of drama "games" for small improvisation groups, placing next to no reliance on sets or props; placing nearly all emphasis, in fact, on environmental awareness and communication.

Games is a collection of classroom interaction activities echoing those of Viola Spolin.

Although *Science World* is just another school magazine on the surface, its project column for 1970-1971 is worthy of great attention from teachers and students alike. Almost every issue for this period presents a basic environmental project, many of them oriented toward the "inventory" concept.

Big Rock Candy Mountain: A Learning to Learn Catalog	Protola Institute, 1115 Merrill St., Menlo Park, Calif. 94025 ($4/issue)

Produced by the people and with the resources of the *Whole Earth Catalog*, *Big Rock Candy Mountain* places special emphasis on environmental education.

The School (II-2)

Davis, James Garrett	*Environmental Planning Recommendations*, Environmental Science Center, 5400 Glenwood Avenue, Golden Valley, Minnesota 55422
Peddiwell, J. Abner	*Saber-Tooth Curriculum*, New York: McGraw-Hill, 1939
Rudd, Robert L.	*Pesticides and the Living Landscape*, Madison: University of Wisconsin Press, 1966

Environmental Planning Recommendations is a collection of practical suggestions for the establishment and use of an outdoor environmental study area at the Blake School in Hopkins, Minnesota. The information is valuable for any school interested in use of the surrounding environment.

Peddiwell's work is a classic study of the problems of meeting environment with curriculum and vice versa. It is as valuable now as it was when first published, perhaps more so.

Rudd's is the best compilation of pesticide information to date for the nonspecialist. The categories of pesticides are examined for their effects on particular forms of life. Well-documented case studies of the most troublesome pest-pesticide problems of the last few years are presented.

New Schools Exchange Newsletter	2940 Hidden Valley La., Santa Barbara, Calif. 93193 ($10/yr.)
This Magazine Is About Schools	56 Esplanade St. East, Suite 301, Toronto 215, Ont., Canada ($3.50/yr.)

These two periodicals provide access to much of the best innovative educational thought on the North American continent.

The District (II-3)

Greenfield, T. B., J. H. House, E. S. Hickcox, and B. H. Buchanan	*Developing School Systems*, Toronto: Ontario Institute for Studies in Education, 1969
McHarg, Ian L.	*Design with Nature*, Garden City, N. Y.: Natural History Press, 1969
Mishan, Ezra J.	*The Costs of Economic Growth*, New York: Praeger, 1967

Developing School Systems is a systems analysis approach to school systems. It is a valuable aid in picturing the system as an environment and as an environmental influence.

For school planning, as for any land-use planning, Ian McHarg's book is a delightful introduction to the capabilities of planners such as himself to make environmentally sensible decisions.

Mishan's book is a semitechnical view of environmental degradation in economic terms. His challenge to the philosophy of unlimited growth is an important one that is receiving ever-wider attention.

The Observers (III-1)

Angyal, Andras	*Foundations for a Science of Personality*, New York: Commonwealth Fund, 1941
Bury, J. B.	*The Idea of Progress*, New York: Dover, 1920
Johnson, Cecil E., ed.	*Human Biology: Contemporary Readings*, Princeton, N. J.
Nash, Roderick, ed.	*The American Environment: Readings in the History of Conservation*, Reading, Mass.: Addison-Wesley, 1968
Nash, Roderick, ed.	*The Call of the Wild (1900–1916)*, New York: Braziller, 1970
Nash, Roderick	*Wilderness and the American Mind*, New Haven: Yale University Press, 1967.
Scientific American	*The Biosphere*, September 1970
Vayda, Andrew P., ed.	*Environment and Cultural Behavior*, Garden City, N. Y.: Natural History Press, 1969

Vayda's work is an extensive collection of anthropological considerations in the field of "human ecology."

Johnson brings together readings on the problem of modern man as a biological phenomenon.

The September 1970 issue of *Scientific American* is another of their excellent "single-topic" efforts. It will probably be published in book form soon.

Bury traced the history of the idea of progress in Western thought. With great insight he describes the impermanence of any guiding "idea" in history and predicts that "progress" will be no different. It is enlightening to see how recently the concept of unlimited growth as progress entered the Western mind.

Wilderness and the American Mind begins with the Old World roots of the first European settlers and continues into the decade of the sixties.

Both Nash's collections trace American ideas of environment and conservation through official and unofficial writings. Though it covers only six years, *The Call of the Wild* is a well-illustrated anthology of the thought and behavior of a very important period.

Andras Angyal presents a stimulating discussion of the "interface" between environment and organism. His psychology is based on the realization that the interface is in no sense defined and is, in reality, an illusion.

The Interpreters (III-2)

Ardrey, Robert	*The Social Contract*, New York: Atheneum, 1970
Eiseley, Loren	*The Firmament of Time*, New York: Atheneum, 1966
Eiseley, Loren	*The Invisible Pyramid*, New York: Scribner's, 1970
Eiseley, Loren	"The Uncompleted Man," *Harper's Magazine*, March 1964
Eiseley, Loren	*The Unexpected Universe*, New York: Harcourt, Brace & World, 1969
Johnson, Cecil E., ed.	*Social and Natural Biology*, Princeton, N. J.: D. Van Nostrand, 1968
Leopold, Aldo	*A Sand County Almanac*, New York: Ballantine, 1949

The Social Contract pursues the all-important and elusive goal of integrating our knowledge of man's biological self with our cultural, philosophic, and political images of man. Ardrey writes, from the center of the storm of controversy over the use and misuse of scientific knowledge, about the very problem of use and misuse. His section on population pressure, "Death by Stress," is particularly good.

Loren Eiseley carves more deeply an expression of the identity of man in nature with every work he writes. In his writing can be seen the inseparability of communication and content. There are few expository writers more worthy of attention from a creative writing class. In "The Uncompleted Man" in particular, Eiseley uses literature, in this case Shakespear's *Macbeth,* to get to the heart of one aspect of man's environmental position. I have used this article as a concluding reading for a course in human ecology for high-school juniors and seniors; it was first presented to me in a secondary-level English class.

Aldo Leopold was one of the most eloquent natural historian-ecologists this country has ever had. His essay on the need for and substance of an ecological ethic is a classic.

Cecil Johnson's book is unexcelled as a collection of environmental interpretation. Some indication of its value may be seen in its list of contributors:

To "Evolution, Eugenics, and Population Perspectives": George Gaylord Simpson, L. S. B. Leakey, Aldous Huxley, John Rock, Garrett Hardin.

To "The Naturalist Biologists": John Steinbeck, Rachel L. Carson, John Muir, John Burroughs, Henry David Thoreau.

To "Animal Behavior": Konrad Lorenz, Nikolass Tinbergen, George B. Schaller, Loren Eiseley.

The Users (III-3)

Bryerton, Gene	*Nuclear Dilemma,* New York: Ballantine, 1970
Cooley, Richard A., and Geoffrey Wandesforde-Smith, eds.	*Congress and the Environment,* Seattle: University of Washington Press, 1970
Dasmann, Raymond F.	*A Different Kind of Country,* New York: Macmillan, 1970
Scientists' Institute for Public Information	Environmental Workbooks, 30 E. 68th St., New York, N. Y. 10021 ($1/copy; $5/all eight)
Swatek, Paul	*The User's Guide to the Protection of the Environment,* New York: Ballantine, 1970

Cooley and Wandesforde-Smith have collected case studies of important environmental legislation, tracing its formation and effects.

A Different Kind of Country, by a leader in ecological conservation, raises important questions in its first sections about the dependence of freedom on a varied environment and the role of the citizen in asserting his rights to such environmental freedom.

The Scientists' Institute for Public Information, publishers of *Environment*, have assembled a group of "workbooks" that provide excellent summaries of practical environmental problems. The nine titles available to date are *Air Pollution; Environmental Cost of Electric Power; Environmental Education, 1970* (higher education); *Environmental Effects of Weapons Technology; Hunger; Nuclear Explosives in Peacetime; Pesticides; Water Pollution*. A tenth title, *Law and the Environment*, may be available soon.

Gene Bryerton's *Nuclear Dilemma* is a case study of the problems encountered in meeting power demands with nuclear power in Eugene, Oregon.

Paul Swatek's *User's Guide* is the best available handbook to practical, everyday environmental considerations. Besides its obvious usefulness in the home, it is no less useful in the classroom. The choice of "User" in the title is informative in itself, for indeed we are using and altering the environment rather than "consuming" it.

Interdisciplinary Study (III-4)

Hardin, Garrett, ed.   *Science, Conflict, and Society*, San Francisco: W. H. Freeman, 1969

Shepard, Paul, and Daniel McKinley   *The Subversive Science*, Boston: Houghton Mifflin, 1969

Just as the environment fits into no single discipline, neither do any of the books listed in this bibliography. Each of them has wide applications dependent on the creativity of the reader. These two works, however, seem to have special value in stimulating interdisciplinary thought.

Shepard and McKinley have brought together the most meaningfully diverse collection of environmental writings to date. The introduction by Paul Shepard is one of the most insightful essays on man's relationship to environment in the literature. The subject headings that provide the books organization may give a clue to its usefulness: "Men as Populations"; "The Environmental Encounter"; "Men and Other Organisms"; "Men in Ecosystems"; "Ethos, Ecos, and Ethics."

Science, Conflict, and Society is a collection of *Scientific American* articles arranged with commentary by Garrett Hardin. Hardin's connecting essays are masterful investigations into the interdisciplinary relationships among diverse subject matters. The collection is built around the following headings: "Scientists and Society"; "The Roots of Social Behavior"; "Population and Heterogeneity"; "What Price Progress?" "War: The Anguish of Renunciation."

Conclusion: Teaching for Survival

Bailey, Liberty Hyde	*The Nature-Study Idea*, New York: Doubleday, Page, and Co., 1903
Dubos, René	"Mere Survival Is not Enough for Man," *Life*, July 24, 1970

Books for the Classroom: All Ages

Grossman, Mary Louise and Shelley and John N. Hamlet	*Our Vanishing Wilderness*, New York: Grossett & Dunlap, 1969
Grossman, Shelley	*Understanding Ecology*, New York: Grossett & Dunlap, 1970
Holling, Holling Clancy	Boston: Houghton Mifflin. *Tree in the Trail; Paddle-to-the-Sea; Minn of the Mississippi; Seabird; Pagoo*
Life Nature Library	New York: Time Incorporated
Life Science Library	New York: Time Incorporated
Our Living World of Nature	New York: McGraw-Hill

Concepts of environmental quality, like concepts of humanity, exist where you find them in children's literature just as in other literature. The writings of Holling Clancy Holling, without once using the term "environment," provide some of the most delightful reading in environmental awareness written for any age. Beautifully illustrated by the author, these books each take "something," whether it be a tree, a carved Indian figure, a turtle, an ivory gull, or a hermit crab, and follow the changes in its environment over the years. They are works of history, biology, anthropology, geography, and each contributes to a deepening sense of environment. They communicate to all ages through pictures and texts which convey a respect for the reader, as well as the subject matter, equaled in few literary works.

The two works by the Grossmans and John Hamlet share many of the same photographs of the American environment. They deal mainly with natural areas and endangered species. *Understanding Ecology* is organized according to ecological concepts and is the easier of the two, as well as being available in paperback. *Our Vanishing Wilderness* takes a "biome" approach and traces the seasons through each of the major life groups in America. The photography is excellent.

The books in the Life Nature Library, written by leaders in the respective fields and recently revised, are a delightful means of introduction to variety in the Earth environment:

Physical environment: *The Earth; The Universe*

Major ecosystems: *The Desert; The Forest; The Mountains; The Poles; The Sea*

Major ecological regions: *Africa; Australia; Eurasia; North America; South America; Tropical Asia*

Major groups of organisms: *The Birds; Early Man; The Fishes; The Insects; The Mammals; The Plants; The Primates; The Reptiles*

Interactions between organisms and environment: *Animal Behavior; Ecology; Evolution*

Index: *A Guide to the Natural World*

The Life Science Library is not of such consistent environmental value as the Nature Library. A few volumes, however, are excellent in their coverage: *Energy; Food and Nutrition; Growth; Health and Disease; Mathematics; Matter; Water; Weather*

Our Living World of Nature is a series produced jointly by the publishers of the World Book Encyclopedia and the United States Department of the Interior. Under the science editorship of Richard B. Fischer of Cornell University and the guidance of an excellent board of consultants, the series is by far the best buy for a classroom ecological library. Each of the volumes is *The Life of* . . . a major ecosystem: *The Cave; The Desert; The Forest; The Jungle; The Marsh; The Mountains; The Ocean; The Pond; Prairies and Plains; Rivers and Streams; Sea Islands; The Seashore*

Books for the Classroom: Secondary

Bates, Marston	*Man in Nature,* Englewood Cliffs, N. J.: Prentice-Hall, 1964
De Bell, Garrett, ed.	*The Environmental Handbook,* New York, N. Y.: Ballantine, 1970
Lauwerys, J. A.	*Man's Impact on Nature,* Garden City, N. Y.: Natural History Press, 1969
Reid, Keith	*Nature's Network,* Garden City, N. Y.: Natural History Press, 1969

For a consideration of man's roots in and relationship to the environment, there is no better short work available than Marston Bates's *Man in Nature.* This relatively inexpensive paperback deals with man as an animal species that has evolved in and been influenced by the environment and that makes use of the environment in ways that create certain environmental problems.

De Bell's *Environmental Handbook,* though prepared for the April 22, 1970, Earth Day, remains of great use as an introduction to environmental problems and environmental thought. It can also be used as a sort of benchmark against which progress in practical environmental improvement can be measured.

The works by Lauwerys and Reid are volumes in the Nature and Science Library of the Natural History Press. Many of the Library's other books are disconcertingly difficult to read and are built around environmental situations in Great Britain, where the majority of them were written. These two stand out as excellent for high-school students. *Nature's Network* is a well-illustrated, well-diagramed introduction to basic ecology. *Man's Impact on Nature* follows fairly closely the format of Bates's book, with illustrations and amplification of details.

Environmental Education

A List of Available Curriculum Materials	Environmental Science Center, 5400 Glenwood Avenue, Golden Valley, Minnesota 55422

Borton, Terry	*Reach, Touch and Teach: Student Concerns and Process Education,* New York: McGraw-Hill, 1970
Swan, Malcolm D., ed.	*Tips and Tricks in Outdoor Education,* Danville, Ill.: Interstate Printers and Publishers, 1970

Tips and Tricks in Outdoor Education is more generally useful than its title implies. Though modest in format, it is probably the best handbook of specifically environmental teaching techniques available. Used in conjunction with Viola Spolin's work and a liberal imagination, this volume could be a tremendous aid to environmental education.

Borton's *Reach, Touch and Teach* is the major publication that has appeared to date from the Affective Development Project, discussed below under "Curricula and Teaching Aids."

Environmental Education	Dembar Educational Research Services, P. O. Box 1605, Madison, Wis. 53701 ($7.50/yr. quarterly)
Nature Study	American Nature Study Society, J. A. Gustafson, R.D. 1, Homer, N. Y. 13077 ($5/yr. quarterly)

Nature Study has a long history, *Environmental Education* is a new publication. Whether either will make important contributions to the development of environmental education during the next few years probably depends mostly on the quality and participation of their readership. With their editorial machinery ready and waiting, it is up to teachers to help them become useful tools by using these journals as forums for ideas in environmental education.

Curricula and Teaching Aids

Biological Sciences Curriculum Study	University of Colorado, P. O. Box 930, Boulder, Colo. 80302
Earth Science Curriculum Project	P. O. Box 1559, Boulder, Colo. 80302
Interaction of Man and the Biosphere	Rand McNally, P. O. Box 7600, Chicago, Ill. 60680

212   *TEACHING FOR SURVIVAL*

Man: A Course of Study	Education Development Center, 15 Mifflin Pl., Cambridge, Mass. 02138
Man the Meaning Maker	Beacon Press, 25 Beacon St., Boston, Mass. 02108
People and Their Environment	Conservation Curriculum Improvement Project, South Carolina Dept. of Education, Chicago: J. G. Ferguson Publishing Co.

The BSCS and ESCP groups are of interest especially because of their current projects along environmental lines. The BSCS is attempting a joint science-social studies text, the ESCP is developing an inner-city environmental education curriculum. Each group publishes a newsletter available from the address listed above.

Interaction of Man and the Biosphere is a junior-high life science text developed by Rand McNally to accompany their previous effort on *Matter and Energy*.

Man: A Course of Study is an elementary course following a format that would be of value at any level. The lives of salmon, herring gulls, baboons, and eskimos are studied with the aim of answering the question, What is human about man?

Man the Meaning Maker is another elementary curricular package that could be put to good use at any grade level. The verbal environment is studied objectively, raising questions of how our perceptions are colored by our capabilities of communication and expression.

People and Their Environment is a set of teacher guides raising environmental questions for classes from K through 12 grades. At the secondary level, the workbooks also branch out into subject areas such as life science, social studies, and home economics.

Affective Development Project	Instructional Services, Affective Development, Rm. 329, Board of Education, 21st St. South of the Parkway, Philadelpnia, Pa. 19103
People	Population Reference Bureau, Columbia Books. 424 Southern Bldg., NW, Washington, D. C. 20005
Plato System of Computer Parameters	Paul Handler, University of Illinois, Urbana, Ill. 61801

One of the strongest efforts to deal with urban environments in education is being carried on by the Affective Development Project of the Philadelphia schools. Samples of materials already developed may be obtained from the office listed above. Terry Borton's work, listed previously under "Environmental Education," is a summary of the group's initial efforts.

People is a small text prepared for late elementary or early junior-high levels by the Population Reference Bureau. It is the bureau's first textbook effort and has the problems of a first effort. It can, however, be a useful tool, and the bureau would appreciate critical comments from teachers as they read or use *People*.

Paul Handler of the physics department of the University of Illinois at Urbana is developing computer programs for use in high schools. An initial project nearing completion covers population dynamics. For schools that have access to computer terminals, this approach to teaching population principles can accomplish what is next to impossible for books or written exercises. The student can literally talk to the computer about population, watching answers to his questions plotted in graphs of population size or structure. A more ambitious project proposed by Dr. Handler is an ecological education program.

***TWO INDISPENSABLE GUIDES TO
WHAT YOU *CAN* DO
TO PROTECT THE ENVIRONMENT***

THE USER'S GUIDE TO THE PROTECTION OF THE ENVIRONMENT

Paul Swatek

The book which tells the reader the daily decisions he can make that will improve or deteriorate his environment—what builds health and which products are potentially dangerous. Which household cleansers contribute the most pollution, and which the least. Brand names, product names, where to get those products which are ecologically safe. This is the everyday action book for environmentally conscious people.

A Friends of the Earth/Ballantine Book $1.25

THE VOTER'S GUIDE TO ENVIRONMENTAL POLITICS

Before, During, and After Election

Edited by Garrett De Bell

Here is the only guide to the major political issues affecting the environment—and what needs to be done and how to get it done through Congress.

your Congressman's voting record on environmental issues

how to tell him what you want him to do in future voting

what issues are before Congress now

the probable consequences of these issues

Exercise your right to vote and your right to a healthy environment!

A Friends of the Earth/Ballantine Book $.95

To order by mail, send price of book plus 5¢ for postage to Dept. CS, Ballantine Books, 36 West 20th Street, New York, N.Y. 10003.

*How to Avoid Poisoning Ourselves
Daily With the Food We Eat*

THE BASIC BOOK OF ORGANIC GARDENING

Edited by Robert Rodale

Now the long-established *Organic Gardening* Magazine and Ballantine Books have produced an original book to guide the unknowledgeable gardener to healthy living through gardening in nature's own way—without pesticides and artificial fertilizers. All the basic information is here:

    What organic gardening is.

    Where organic gardening supplies can be obtained.

    How to prepare the soil, compost, mulch, etc.

    Why gardening organically is essential to the protection of the environment.

An *Organic Gardening*®/Ballantine Book $1.25

To order by mail send price of book plus 5¢ for postage to Dept. CS, Ballantine Books, 36 West 20th Street, N. Y., N. Y. 10003

*A powerful, provocative book
for those who care about
what tomorrow might bring ...*

Moment in the Sun

Robert and Leona Train Rienow

A report on the Deteriorating Quality of the American Environment

"A VERY IMPORTANT BOOK . . . We've been told for some years now that the wide open spaces are getting narrower all the time, and quicker than some of us might think. The authors of this book lay it right on the line . . . after reading this sane and humane book, one wants to plead with everybody to keep aware, and not regard these things as part of some inevitable black comedy."

—*Harper's Magazine*

A Sierra Club-Ballantine Book   95¢

To order by mail, enclose price of book plus 5¢ a copy for handling and send to Dept. CS, Ballantine Books, 36 West 20th Street, New York, N.Y. 10003.

A stunning, angry report that will grow in importance with each new ocean disaster

The Frail Ocean

Wesley Marx

"A fascinating and important book. The obvious comparison is with Rachel Carson's "Silent Spring," and I can only hope Mr. Marx's book will be as widely read, and have a comparable impact."
—*The New York Times*

A Sierra Club-Ballantine Book 95¢

To order by mail, enclose price of book plus 5¢ a copy for handling, and send to Dept. CS, Ballantine Books, 36 West 20th Street, New York, N.Y. 10003